Unit Test Frameworks

Other Resources from O'Reilly

Related titles   JUnit Pocket Guide   Extreme Programming Pocket
                     NUnit Pocket Reference   Guide

                                                       Java Extreme Programming
                                                       Cookbook

oreilly.com   *oreilly.com* is more than a complete catalog of O'Reilly books. You'll also find links to news, events, articles, weblogs, sample chapters, and code examples.

oreillynet.com is the essential portal for developers interested in open and emerging technologies, including new platforms, programming languages, and operating systems.

Conferences   O'Reilly brings diverse innovators together to nurture the ideas that spark revolutionary industries. We specialize in documenting the latest tools and systems, translating the innovator's knowledge into useful skills for those in the trenches. Visit *conferences.oreilly.com* for our upcoming events.

Safari Bookshelf (*safari.oreilly.com*) is the premier online reference library for programmers and IT professionals. Conduct searches across more than 1,000 books. Subscribers can zero in on answers to time-critical questions in a matter of seconds. Read the books on your Bookshelf from cover to cover or simply flip to the page you need. Try it today with a free trial.

Unit Test Frameworks

Paul Hamill

O'REILLY®

Beijing · Cambridge · Farnham · Köln · Paris · Sebastopol · Taipei · Tokyo

Unit Test Frameworks
by Paul Hamill

Published by O'Reilly Media, Inc., 1005 Gravenstein Highway North, Sebastopol, CA 95472.

O'Reilly books may be purchased for educational, business, or sales promotional use. Online editions are also available for most titles (*safari.oreilly.com*). For more information, contact our corporate/institutional sales department: (800) 998-9938 or *corporate@oreilly.com*.

Editor:	Mike Hendrickson
Production Editor:	Mary Brady
Cover Designer:	Ellie Volckhausen
Interior Designer:	Melanie Wang

Printing History:

November 2004:   First Edition.

 This book uses RepKover,™ a durable and flexible lay-flat binding.

ISBN: 0-596-00689-6
[M]

Table of Contents

Preface

This book presents a comprehensive review of the xUnit family of unit test frameworks, including their usage, architecture, and theory. We begin by building a simple unit test framework from the ground up. The xUnit architecture is presented, using the JUnit framework as the reference implementation of xUnit. We progressively build an example application to demonstrate common practices and patterns of unit test development. Several popular versions of xUnit, including JUnit, CppUnit, NUnit, PyUnit, and XMLUnit, are covered in detail. Detailed class references are provided for JUnit and CppUnit as appendixes.

As a software development methodology, unit testing incorporates many rules and guidelines. However, writing unit tests is an art, not a science. Once you are familiar with the unit test driven approach to development, rigidly following its rules is optional. The true value of unit testing is in the focus on low-level software quality it gives developers, rather than as a formal process.

Audience

This book is intended for software developers, technical managers, and quality assurance staff who are learning about unit testing and agile development. Agile development is the wave of the future in software engineering, and many technical organizations are adopting it. Using unit test frameworks to enable test driven development is a key to becoming agile.

Contents of This Book

Here is a summary of the topics covered in each chapter and appendix:

Chapter 1, *Unit Test Frameworks: An Overview*
   An overview that explains what unit test frameworks are and how they are used.

Chapter 2, *Getting Started: Tutorial*

A tutorial that creates a simple Java test framework. This provides the fundamentals of how unit test frameworks work. Appendix A contains the C++ version of this simple framework tutorial.

Chapter 3, *The xUnit Family of Unit Test Frameworks*

A review of xUnit, using JUnit as a reference implementation to demonstrate basic xUnit architecture and usage.

Chapter 4, *Writing Unit Tests*

An overview of writing unit tests. This offers a more detailed discussion of different types of unit tests and patterns of unit test development.

Chapter 5, *Unit Testing GUI Applications*

A discussion of unit testing of GUI applications. This chapter explains how to build and test GUI objects following the smart object model.

Chapter 6, *JUnit*

A description of the details of the usage and architecture of JUnit for Java.

Chapter 7, *CppUnit*

A description of the details of the usage and architecture of CppUnit for C++.

Chapter 8, *NUnit*

A description of the details of the usage and architecture for NUnit for .NET.

Chapter 9, *PyUnit*

A description of the details of the usage and architecture of PyUnit for Python.

Chapter 10, *XMLUnit*

A description of the details of the usage and architecture of XMLUnit for XML.

Chapter 11, *Resources*

A list of additional resources for unit test frameworks and related topics.

Appendix A, *Simple C++ Unit Test Framework*

The C++ version of the simple unit test framework from Chapter 2.

Appendix B, *JUnit Class Reference*

A detailed class reference for JUnit's key package junit.framework.

Appendix C, *CppUnit Class Reference*

A detailed class reference for CppUnit.

Glossary

A list of definitions for important technical terms used in this book.

Conventions Used in This Book

The following typographical conventions are used in this book:

Plain text
> Indicates regular text and descriptions.

Constant width
> Indicates commands, methods, attributes, data types, class names, or the output from commands. It also shows the actual source code.

Italic
> Indicates new terms where they are defined, pathnames, file directories, filenames, and Internet names, such as email addresses, and URLs.

Constant Width Bold
> Indicates source code that is being emphasized for your attention.

Code in this book is formatted as shown here to distinguish it from the rest of the text. Code examples begin with the filename where the code resides.

```
MyClass.java
public class MyClass {

    myMethod( ) {
        int id = 3;
    }

}
```

Using Code Examples

This book is here to help you get your job done. In general, you may use the code in this book in your programs and documentation. You do not need to contact us for permission unless you're reproducing a significant portion of the code. For example, writing a program that uses several chunks of code from this book does not require permission. Selling or distributing a CD-ROM of examples from O'Reilly books does require permission. Answering a question by citing this book and quoting example code does not require permission. Incorporating a significant amount of example code from this book into your product's documentation does require permission.

We appreciate, but do not require, attribution. An attribution usually includes the title, author, publisher, and ISBN. For example: *"Unit Test Frameworks,* by Paul Hamill. Copyright 2005 O'Reilly Media, Inc., 0-596-00689-6."

If you feel your use of code examples falls outside fair use or the permission given above, feel free to contact us at *permissions@oreilly.com.*

How to Contact Us

Please address comments and questions concerning this book to the publisher:

O'Reilly Media, Inc.
1005 Gravenstein Highway North
Sebastopol, CA 95472
(800) 998-9938 (in the United States or Canada)
(707) 829-0515 (international or local)
(707) 829-0104 (fax)

We have a web page for this book, where we list errata, examples, and any additional information. You can access this page at:

http://www.oreilly.com/catalog/unitest/

To comment or ask technical questions about this book, send email to:

bookquestions@oreilly.com

For more information about our books, conferences, Resource Centers, and the O'Reilly Network, see our web site at:

http://www.oreilly.com

Acknowledgments

My sincere thanks go out to my reviewers: Ron Jeffries, James Newkirk, Philip Plumlee, J. B. Rainsberger, Simon Robbie, and Anthony Williams. Their shared experience and advice was incredibly useful and encouraging. This book could not have been completed without their help.

This book is built on the work of software pioneers. Kent Beck is the original author of the xUnit architecture in the form of SmalltalkUnit. Ward Cunningham, Kent Beck, and Ron Jeffries are the formulators of the Extreme Programming methodology, which led to many of the test driven development practices described in this book. Erich Gamma and Kent Beck ported SmalltalkUnit to Java to create JUnit, the most widely used and extended unit test framework. Many individual developers created and contributed to the different versions of xUnit, which are classic examples of open source software, built by the collective efforts of the software development community. The fingerprints of these talented engineers are all over the material covered by this book.

CHAPTER 1

Unit Test Frameworks: An Overview

Most people who write software have at least some experience with unit testing. If you have ever written a few lines of throwaway code just to try something out, you've built a unit test. On the other end of the software spectrum, many large-scale applications have huge batteries of test cases that are repeatedly run and added to throughout the development process. Unit tests are useful at all levels of programming.

What are unit test frameworks and how are they used? Simply stated, they are software tools to support writing and running unit tests, including a foundation on which to build tests and the functionality to execute the tests and report their results. They are not solely tools for testing; they can also be used as development tools on a par with preprocessors and debuggers. Unit test frameworks can contribute to almost every stage of software development, including software architecture and design, code implementation and debugging, performance optimization, and quality assurance.

Unit tests usually are developed concurrently with production code, but are not built into the final software product. The relationship of unit tests to production code is shown in Figure 1-1.

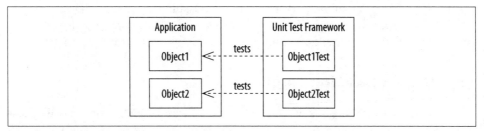

Figure 1-1. Production application and unit test framework

An application is built from software objects linked together. The unit tests use the application's objects, but exist inside the unit test framework. This approach has a number of nice aspects. The production code is not cluttered up with built-in unit tests. The size of the compiled application tends to be kept smaller for the same reason. The tests can be run separately from the application, so the objects can be tested in isolation.

A single unit test should test a particular behavior within the production code. Its success or failure validates a single unit of code. Well-written tests set up an environment or scenario that is independent of any other conditions, then perform a distinct action and check a definite result. These tests should avoid dependencies on the results of other tests (called *test coupling*), and they should be short and simple. By starting with tests of the most basic functionality, then gradually building to tests of compound objects and behaviors, a unit test framework can be used to verify very complex architectures. Having such a test framework to build upon not only is much easier than developing standalone tests, but also produces more thorough, effective tests. A comprehensive suite of unit tests enables rapid application development, since the effects of every change can be immediately and thoroughly verified.

In the traditional jargon of testing, tests are categorized as *black box* or *white box*, depending on the amount of access to the internal workings of whatever is being tested. *Functional* and *structural* tests are related ideas. For example, a test that simply runs a program and checks its return code is a black box (functional) test, since nothing is known about how the program is written. Unit tests are usually white box (structural) tests, since the test framework is able to access the internal structure of the code being tested. Most object-oriented languages provide access protection, preventing outside classes from accessing protected or private code elements. Because of this, unit tests often are written to test only the public interfaces of the objects tested. This encourages the design of objects with discrete, testable interfaces and a minimum of complex hidden behavior. Thus, writing testable objects promotes good object-oriented development practices.

Another distinction is drawn between *programmer* and *acceptance tests*. Developers write programmer tests as they design and build code. These usually test low-level code elements, such as methods and interfaces. Acceptance tests may be specified or written by a nonprogrammer, such as a quality-assurance person or product manager. These generally are functional tests of high-level behavior, such as producing output or performing a user task. Unit tests may fall into either of these categories.

Test Driven Development

Unit test frameworks are a key element of Test Driven Development (TDD), also known as "test-first programming." TDD is one of the most significant and widely used practices in Extreme Programming (XP) and other Agile Development methodologies. Test frameworks achieve their maximum utility when used to enable TDD, although they still are useful when TDD is not followed. This book concentrates on unit test frameworks as a family of tools, rather than specifically on TDD, but the two topics are closely related.

The key rule of TDD can be summarized as "test twice, code once," by analogy to the carpenter's rule of "measure twice, cut once." "Test twice, code once" refers to the three-step procedure involved in any code change:

1. Write a test of the new code and see it fail.
2. Write the new code, doing "the simplest thing that could possibly work."
3. See the test succeed, and refactor the code.

These three basic steps are the *TDD cycle*.

Step 1 is to write a test, run it, and verify the resulting failure. The failure is important because it validates that the test fails as expected. It is often tempting to skip running the test and seeing the failure. Don't.

In Step 2, code is written to make the test succeed. A wise guideline is doing "the simplest thing that could possibly work." This may be a completely trivial implementation, such as having the new code return a constant value or copying and pasting code from one place to another. It doesn't have to be pretty; it just has to pass the test. The temptation in this step is to do a little extra work and make some additional code change not directly related to passing the test. Again, don't do this.

In Step 3, the test succeeds, verifying both the new code and its test. At this point, the new code may be refactored. *Refactoring* is a software engineering concept defined as "behavior-preserving transformation." More formally, refactoring is the process of transforming code to improve its internal design without changing its external functionality. Within the TDD cycle, refactoring starts with the inelegant code that was written to pass the unit test and improves it by removing duplication or other ugliness. Since the unit test is in place, the details of how the code is implemented can be altered with confidence.

New code should only be written when a test fails. Code changes are only expected to occur when you are refactoring, adding new functionality, or debugging. Continuously repeating the TDD cycle is the most atomic level of the software development process. Software changes generally fall under two categories: adding new functionality or fixing bugs.

When adding new functionality, the first step is always to write a unit test that anticipates and uses the new code. After the unit test runs and fails, add the new code and re-test to verify success. The unit test has value aside from simply demonstrating that the new functionality works. Writing the test forces you to think in advance about the ideal design of the new code. Thus, in a sneaky and subtle way, TDD makes all new development part of a methodical, low-level software design process. Once the new unit test and functionality are in place, the unit test serves as the definitive, working example of how the new code is supposed to be used. For these reasons, time spent writing unit tests is not solely testing effort. Investments in testing are equal investments in design.

When debugging, you should first write a unit test that fails because of the bug. This is a useful effort in itself, because it determines exactly how the bug occurs. Once the unit test is in place and failing, fix the bug and re-run the test to verify that the bug is closed. Aside from fixing the bug, this process has the additional benefit of creating a test that will catch it. If the bug is ever re-introduced, the test will fail and highlight the problem.

By following the TDD cycle, you can come as close as humanly possible to writing flawless code on the first try—in other words, "code once." The process gives you a clear indication that a piece of work is done. When a new unit test is written and then fails, the task is halfway completed. You cannot move on to something else until the test succeeds.

Unit Testing and Quality Assurance

Unit test frameworks are valuable when used for automated software testing as part of a quality assurance (QA) process. In many software development groups, the QA process starts when new code is submitted, built, and unit tested. Often, the unit tests include not only programmer tests, but also acceptance tests designed or written by the QA team. If all the unit tests succeed, the code is provisionally accepted and sent to a QA engineer for inspection and testing.

Running the full suite of unit tests as the first step in QA has many benefits. Most importantly, the tests ensure that the code is solid the moment it has left the developers' hands. No human intervention is required to run the tests and evaluate the results. Either they all succeed, or there is a failure. Such Boolean (true/false) results are ideal because an automated system can understand them. The success of the unit tests confirms that the developers' assumptions are valid, and that the low-level functionality is working correctly at a level of scrutiny that functional tests can never achieve. When numerous developers are making changes at once, the unit tests provide confidence that nobody's changes caused someone else's code to break. Furthermore, unit tests help to provide accountability. Knowing exactly which test fails usually makes it apparent whose change broke things. "Breaking the build" once meant submitting code that caused a compile to fail, but now often refers to causing a unit test failure as well. Many teams employ heinous punishments (such as making the responsible developer buy donuts or beer for coworkers) to remind everyone that breaking the build is a serious offense. The failure of a unit test clearly places a high priority on fixing the problem. If TDD is followed rigorously, the code should never be left in a state in which a unit test fails.

Unit testing doesn't replace all other types of testing. It is entirely possible to develop thoroughly unit-tested, completely bulletproof code that is lacking in usability and performance. Stress testing, performance testing, and usability testing usually are separate considerations from unit testing. QA effort is still necessary to try out the completed application, decide whether it performs acceptably in real-world conditions, observe how things work outside of a controlled development environment, and otherwise apply human judgment. There are elements of software functionality for which it is difficult or impossible to write good unit tests. These include GUI "look and feel," responses to system events, interaction with distributed application components, and many other possibilities. Sometimes unit tests can be written to simulate these types of situations, but ultimately, there is no substitute for reality or for a user's objective feedback.

Although manual QA testing is still important, unit tests are a powerful tool for QA. Developers who use test-centric development report dramatic improvements in software quality, speed of development, and ability to make significant design changes on the fly. These speed and quality advantages rapidly become apparent from the QA perspective as well.

Homegrown Unit Testing

Writing simple tests comes naturally to most programmers. The classic beginner exercise of writing a three-line program that prints "Hello world!" is a basic unit test of the development language and environment. Find a software shop with no unit test framework in place (if such a prehistoric place could possibly exist), and you may see developers writing their own little "toy programs" or "test utilities" to try out new code. The sad thing about this approach is that the toy programs are thrown away once the developer is done with them. Later, when something breaks, someone has to laboriously debug the production code, without benefit of the developer's test.

Another common low-level testing technique is to build tests into the production code with ASSERT macros. In debug builds, the macro tests a condition and sends a message if it fails. In release builds, the macro is defined to be empty, so no test code is included. This allows a developer to sprinkle assertions throughout the code, reporting any condition that is worthy of someone's attention. Asserts can be a useful thing to have in your software toolbox, but far less so than true unit testing. For an assert to be evaluated, the production code must be run to the point where it is defined. It's not convenient for automated testing, since an automated system doesn't know how to cause a particular assert to fire. Failures don't leave the developer with a clear path to correct the problem. Fixing a failure is no guarantee that the same problem will not happen again under different circumstances. Reliance on testing with this type of assert is unlikely to produce high-quality software. It is a forerunner to formal unit testing, which uses test asserts contained within well-defined tests, rather than placed randomly in the production code.

Just as many developers take the initiative and write test programs to try out small pieces of code, it's common to find developers putting together basic, home-grown unit test frameworks that take care of their testing needs. As demonstrated in the Chapter 2, a test framework can be just a few lines of code to run unit tests and report the results. Even a very simple framework can be the foundation for thorough testing of complex applications.

Getting Started: Tutorial

Software concepts are best explained by example. In this tutorial, you will set up a simple unit test framework and use it to help build a basic application. Following the primary rule of TDD, every change to the code is preceded by a unit test.

Why build our own test framework, instead of starting with one of the xUnits? The xUnit test frameworks are powerful tools. They not only support writing unit tests, running them, and reporting the results, but also include test classes, helper code, test runners, and utilities. Such features minimize the amount of code required to write a unit test and maximize your ability to test complex code. They include much more than the minimum needed to build unit tests.

The core functionality of running tests and reporting the results is fundamentally simple. Developers working in cross-platform environments, using older compilers or uncommon languages or needing closer control over how unit tests and their results are handled may not be able to use the xUnits or want to invest the time to set them up. The proliferation of very basic unit test frameworks available online demonstrates the popular belief that "simpler is better" when it comes to unit test frameworks. Most importantly, creating your own framework clearly demonstrates how unit tests work and how straightforward the unit test framework concept really is.

The example code is given in Java. Appendix A contains the C++ version. The code can be found on the CD accompanying this book in the directory */examples/ chapter2*. Consider entering the code in this chapter by hand as if you were coding it from scratch. It's an illuminating exercise that will help you to understand how quick and easy it is to set up and start using a unit test framework.

This tutorial assumes that you have a Java runtime environment and compiler installed. Sun's *javac* compiler is recommended, as is the GNU *gcj* Java compiler. Versions of both compilers are readily available for most platforms.

The step-by-step procedures given here assume that you are compiling and running the code from the command line. If you are using a graphical Integrated Development Environment (IDE), the details of how you build and run the example code will differ.

Outline of an Application: the Virtual Library

This book presents an increasingly complex series of code examples to illustrate unit test framework usage. The examples fit into an overall system concept. Your mission, should you choose to accept it, is to build a system for managing a library full of books. Books will have the attributes you might expect, such as title and author. Users of the system will need to be able to perform a variety of library operations: adding new books, searching for books, checking them in and out of the library, and so forth.

Example 1: Create a Book

For the first example, we will create a representation of a book and its title. Since we'll do test-first development, we need to set up a unit test framework prior to writing any code for the book class. This test framework serves both as the foundation for the example's unit tests and also as an illustration of just how simple a functional test framework can be. Building it is Step 0.

The subsequent steps are the usual three steps in the TDD cycle. Step 1 is to write a unit test to verify that a book has been created. At first, the unit test will fail, because the functionality to create a book does not yet exist. Step 2 is to build the functionality to create a book. In Step 3, the test succeeds, proving that the functionality works and providing an example of how to use it.

Step 0: Set Up the Unit Test Framework

The unit test framework initially is built on a single class, UnitTest, shown in Figure 2-1.

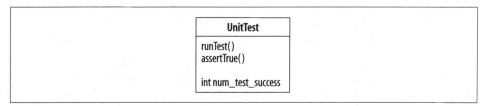

Figure 2-1. The class UnitTest

The source code for UnitTest is given in Example 2-1.

Example 2-1. The base class UnitTest

```
UnitTest.java
public abstract class UnitTest {

    protected static int num_test_success = 0;
```

Example 2-1. The base class UnitTest (continued)

```
    public abstract void runTest( ) throws Exception;

    protected void assertTrue( boolean condition, String msg )
        throws Exception {
        if (!condition)
            throw new Exception(msg);
        num_test_success++;
    }

}
```

The class UnitTest is abstract because its purpose is to be the parent class for actual unit tests. It contains a static integer member, num_test_success, which keeps track of the number of successful tests. Descendant classes override the method runTest( ) to run actual tests. The method assertTrue( ) tests a condition. If the condition is TRUE, the successful test counter is incremented. If it is FALSE, an Exception is thrown containing a message string associated with the condition.

Compile UnitTest with the command javac UnitTest.java (or your compiler's equivalent command). Believe it or not, you now have a simple but functional test framework with which to start building tests.

You could look at this unit test framework and ask, "How is something that can be written in 10 lines of code worth an entire book?" Unit test frameworks are fundamentally simple tools that can be used in sophisticated ways. The xUnit frameworks represent significantly more complicated and powerful pieces of software than the basic framework used in this example. In the subsequent chapters, we will get into the features of more advanced unit test frameworks and how they save coding effort and enable building more complex tests.

Step 1: Create a Unit Test

Now that you have built your simple unit test framework, it's time to create a unit test. The unit test will fail because the functionality it tests has not been built. Remember the TDD process: if your tests do not fail initially, then you are not writing good tests. The test failure also demonstrates that the framework works as expected.

Before writing the first test, take a moment to decide what you want the new code to do and how to test whether it succeeds. We want to represent a book and its title, which sensibly is done with a class named Book having a title attribute. So, we will create a unit test that creates an instance of Book and checks its title.

Example 2-2 shows the implementation of the first unit test, BookTest.

Example 2-2. The unit test class BookTest

BookTest.java
```
public class BookTest extends UnitTest {

    public void runTest() throws Exception {
        Book book = new Book("Dune");
        assertTrue(book.title.equals("Dune"), "checking title");
    }

}
```

BookTest is very simple. It creates a book, giving the title as an argument to the constructor. It then tests that the value of the attribute title has been set correctly. The string checking title describes the test condition.

Compile this new class. The compiler will inform you that it does not know about a class named Book. So, create the most basic implementation of Book that will allow everything to compile, as shown in Example 2-3.

Example 2-3. The class Book

Book.java
```
public class Book {

    public String title = "";

    Book(String title) {}

}
```

Someone who cares about software design would have a problem with this code. Making the title attribute public is not good; it would be better to make it private and provide an accessor function such as getTitle() to obtain its value. However, adding the accessor now would create two methods that should be unit tested: the constructor and the accessor. This change should wait until the current change is done and tested.

Book and BookTest can now compile. Our first unit test is now built. We still need to run the test to see whether it succeeds or fails. One additional new piece of code is necessary. The class TestRunner runs BookTest and reports success or failure. Example 2-4 gives the implementation of TestRunner.

Example 2-4. The class TestRunner

TestRunner.java
```
public class TestRunner {

    public static void main(String[] args) {
        TestRunner tester = new TestRunner();
    }
```

Example 2-4. The class TestRunner (continued)

```
public TestRunner() {
    try {
        UnitTest test = new BookTest();
        test.runTest();
        System.out.println("SUCCESS!");
    }
    catch (Exception e) {
        e.printStackTrace();
        System.out.println("FAILURE!");
    }
}
}
```

TestRunner contains the main() method for the test framework. When an instance of TestRunner is created, it creates a BookTest and calls its runTest() method. If there is no error, success is reported. If an exception is thrown, TestRunner reports the location of the failure from the exception stack trace.

Compile the new code and run it using java TestRunner. You should get the following results:

```
FAILURE!
java.lang.Exception: checking title
        at UnitTest.assertTrue(UnitTest.java:10)
        at BookTest.runTest(BookTest.java:5)
        at TestRunner.<init>(TestRunner.java:10)
        at TestRunner.main(TestRunner.java:4)
```

A failure is reported. The test description is printed, followed by the stack trace showing where the failure occurred.

Congratulations! You have produced a test failure. This failure is a success of the TDD process. The unit test BookTest has done its job, reporting that the functionality being tested is not implemented. The simple framework has performed its role, running the test and reporting the results, including the location and description of the failure. We now have a working unit test framework.

A semantic distinction is drawn between failures and errors in unit testing. A failure is a unit test reporting that a test condition has evaluated to false. If you're not producing failures, you're not writing good tests. An error is an unexpected problem, such as an uncaught exception. Errors may happen, but producing them is not a goal of the TDD process.

Step 2: Create a Book

In the previous step, we wrote the first unit test, BookTest. In order to get BookTest to compile, we also created a basic implementation of the class Book. When run, BookTest still fails, because Book does not yet contain the functionality being tested.

In this step, we add the necessary code to get the test to succeed. As compared to Step 1, the changes required at this point are very minor.

The class Book is modified so that the title attribute is set in the constructor, as shown in Example 2-5.

Example 2-5. The class Book with title attribute set by the constructor

Book.java
```
public class Book {

    public String title = "";

    Book(String title) { this.title = title; }

}
```

Step 3: Test Again

The final step is to rebuild the code, re-run the unit test, and see whether the changes produce the desired results.

Compile the code and run it using java TestRunner. You should see the following result:

```
SUCCESS!
```

Mission accomplished! Creating a class representing a book with a title attribute is a simple task that most developers could accomplish in a few minutes, without feeling the need for a unit test to validate it. However, we accomplished much more than that in this exercise. We created a simple unit test framework, built a unit test, and validated that the framework behaves as expected in both failure and success cases. The initial unit test, although a trivial validation of the class Book, is important as a test of the framework itself.

From the formal software design perspective, the class architecture we've just built is shown in Figure 2-2.

Example 2: Create a Library

For the second example, we'll add additional functionality to the library application. The new features will allow us to create a library, add a book to it, and get a book from it. Along the way, we also will add a few features to the unit test framework.

Consider the minimum new code that will provide what is necessary. Creating a library is easy. We can instantiate an empty class called Library and be done. Adding a book to the library is a feature with a little more to think through. We have a class Book, and the fact that we can add a Book to a Library suggests how a Library should work. A Library contains Books. The ability to get a book from the library reinforces this idea.

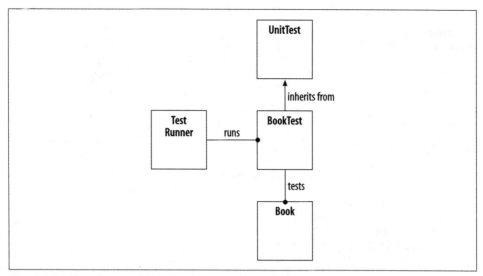

Figure 2-2. Class diagram for the basic unit test framework

Let's create a unit test that adds a Book to a Library and then gets the Book back out again, verifying that the Library contains the Book.

Step 1: Test adding a Book to a Library

The class LibraryTest is the initial unit test for the Library class. Its implementation is shown in Example 2-6.

Example 2-6. Initial version of LibraryTest

LibraryTest.java
```
public class LibraryTest extends UnitTest {

    public void runTest() throws Exception {
        Library library = new Library();
        Book expectedBook = new Book( "Dune" );
        library.addBook( expectedBook );
        Book actualBook = library.getBook( "Dune" );
        assertTrue( actualBook.title.equals("Dune"), "got book" );
    }

}
```

The test creates a Library and a Book, adds the Book to the Library, then gets the Book from the Library and asserts that the expected Book was found.

Additional code must be added to TestRunner to run LibraryTest, as shown in Example 2-7.

Example 2-7. TestRunner modified to run LibraryTest

TestRunner.java
```
public class TestRunner {

    public static void main(String[] args) {
        TestRunner tester = new TestRunner();
    }

    public TestRunner() {
        try {
            BookTest test = new BookTest();
            test.runTest();
            LibraryTest test2 = new LibraryTest();
            test2.runTest();
            System.out.println("SUCCESS!");
        }
        catch (Exception e) {
            System.out.println("FAILURE!");
            e.printStackTrace();
        }
        System.out.println( UnitTest.getNumSuccess()
            + " tests completed successfully" );
    }
}
```

Now that more than one unit test is being run, it's useful to report the value of the test success counter. To obtain this value, the accessor function getNumSuccess( ) is added to the class UnitTest, as shown in Example 2-8.

Example 2-8. UnitTest with accessor function getNumSuccess

UnitTest.java
```
public abstract class UnitTest {

    protected static int num_test_success = 0;

    public abstract void runTest() throws Exception;

    public static int getNumSuccess()
        { return num_test_success; }

    protected void assertTrue(boolean condition, String msg)
        throws Exception {
        if (!condition)
            throw new Exception(msg);
        num_test_success++;
    }

}
```

So far, the code will not compile because there's no class named Library. Let's create the most basic implementation that will allow LibraryTest to compile, as shown in Example 2-9.

Example 2-9. Initial version of the class Library

Library.java
```
public class Library {

   Library() {}

   public void addBook( Book book ) {}

   public Book getBook( String title ) {
      return new Book("");
   }
}
```

The code should now compile and run. The framework should report the failure of LibraryTest, as well as the success of BookTest:

```
FAILURE!
java.lang.Exception: got book
        at UnitTest.assertTrue(UnitTest.java:13)
        at LibraryTest.runTest(LibraryTest.java:11)
        at TestRunner.<init>(TestRunner.java:12)
        at TestRunner.main(TestRunner.java:4)
1 tests completed successfully
```

Step 2: Add a Book to a Library

Now it's time to add the functionality to make LibraryTest succeed. We should only have to change the Library class. If any other changes were necessary, it would suggest that the unit test relies on some behavior other than what Library provides.

You might already have a design in mind for Library that uses some kind of collection to store a set of Books. You could start building it at this point. But consider this: Library can be made to pass LibraryTest without using a collection. Since we should not be building any functionality without first writing a unit test for it, implementing a collection of Books is going too far. Stick to the principle of doing "the simplest thing that could possibly work."

Example 2-10 shows the Library class with new functionality to pass LibraryTest.

Example 2-10. Library with changes to pass LibraryTest

Library.java
```
public class Library {

   private Book book;
```

Example 2-10. Library with changes to pass LibraryTest (continued)

```
Library( ) {}

public void addBook( Book book ) {
    this.book = book;
}

public Book getBook( String title ) {
    return book;
}

}
```

The Library class now contains a data member: a single Book. This may seem like cheating. After all, we certainly want a library to be able to hold more than one item. But LibraryTest tests only adding and retrieving a single Book, so the code given here is the minimum necessary to pass the test. Before implementing a Library that can contain multiple Books, add a new unit test to LibraryTest to test that behavior.

Step 3: Check Unit Test Results

Compiling and running this code should demonstrate success for both of the unit tests:

```
SUCCESS!
2 tests completed successfully
```

The architecture of our unit test framework, unit tests, and production classes is shown in Figure 2-3.

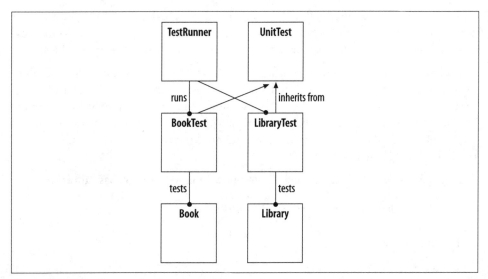

Figure 2-3. Class diagram for the unit test framework and unit tests

The current implementation of Library is trivial. While writing the code to pass LibraryTest, we realized that it could be satisfied with a Library that contains a single book. So, the obvious unit test to write next is one that tests adding and retrieving multiple Books from the Library. Often, adding one unit test and the corresponding functionality makes it clear what the next step should be. Since you are building a series of unit tests as you go and constantly validating the new code, you can be confident that everything you've built is working, and rapidly make changes. Sometimes you will find that a trivial implementation put in place just to get a unit test to pass stays in place for many iterations of the software. That's fine! This is the process working to save you from building unnecessary code.

You might already have decided there are flaws in Library and Book. For example, Library's getBook() method returns an uninitialized Book if it is called before addBook(). The class Book has a public attribute, title, which should be made private and accessed with a get method. How should you take care of such problems? Write tests that fail because of these problems, then write code that fixes them. Every time you come up with a potential change to the design, there is a clear process for trying it out. Test first, then code, then test again.

CHAPTER 3

The xUnit Family of Unit Test Frameworks

Kent Beck published a unit test framework for the Smalltalk language in 1999. The architecture of SmalltalkUnit (or SUnit) represents a sweet spot, an ideal balance between simplicity and utility. Later, Erich Gamma ported SUnit to Java, creating JUnit. JUnit in turn begat CppUnit, NUnit, PyUnit, XMLUnit, and ports to many other languages. A dizzying array of unit test frameworks built on the same model now exists. These frameworks are known as the xUnit family of tools. All are free, open source software.

xUnit Family Members

Some of the most popular xUnit test frameworks are listed next, with brief summaries of their target language and testing domain. This is just a sample of the many xUnit-derived test tools.

JUnit
> The reference implementation of xUnit, JUnit is by far the most widely used and extended unit test framework. It is implemented in and used with Java and is covered in Chapter 6 of this book.

CppUnit
> The C++ port of JUnit, it closely follows the JUnit model. This is covered in Chapter 7 of this book.

NUnit
> The xUnit for .NET. Rather than being a direct port of JUnit, it has a .NET-specific implementation that generally follows the xUnit model. It is written in C# and can be used to test any .NET language, including C#, VB.Net, J#, and Managed C++. It is covered in Chapter 8 of this book.

PyUnit
> The Python version of xUnit. It is included as a standard component of Python 2.1, and is covered in Chapter 9 of this book.

SUnit

Also known as SmalltalkUnit, this is the original xUnit, and the basis of the xUnit architecture. It is written in and used with the Smalltalk language.

vbUnit

vbUnit is xUnit for Visual Basic (VB). It is written in VB and supports building unit tests in VB and COM development.

utPLSQL

utPLSQL is xUnit for Oracle's PL/SQL language. It is written in and used with PL/SQL.

MinUnit

A great example of a minimal but functional unit test framework. It is implemented in three lines of C and is used to test C code.

xUnit Extensions

Beyond the xUnits themselves, many add-on tools are available that extend the functionality of existing unit test frameworks into specialized domains, rather than acting as standalone tools. A representative set of popular extensions is listed here.

XMLUnit

An xUnit extension to support XML testing. Versions exist as extensions to both JUnit and NUnit. This is covered in Chapter 10 of this book.

JUnitPerf

A JUnit extension that supports writing code performance and scalability tests. It is written in and used with Java.

Cactus

A JUnit extension for unit testing server-side code such as servlets, JSPs, or EJBs. It is written in and used with Java.

JFCUnit

A JUnit extension that supports writing GUI tests for Java Swing applications. It is written in and used with Java.

NUnitForms

An NUnit extension that supports GUI tests of Windows Forms applications. It is written in C# and can be used with any .NET language.

HTMLUnit

An extension to JUnit that tests web-based applications. It simulates a web browser, and is oriented towards writing tests that deal with HTML pages.

HTTPUnit

Another JUnit extension that tests web-based applications. It is oriented towards writing tests that deal with HTTP request and response objects.

Jester

A helpful extension to JUnit that automatically finds and reports code that is not covered by unit tests. Versions exist for Python (Pester) and NUnit (Nester). Many other code coverage tools with similar functionality exist.

The xUnit Architecture

The xUnits all have the same basic architecture. This section describes the xUnit fundamentals, using JUnit as the reference example, since it is the most widely used of the xUnits. The other xUnits vary in their implementation details, but follow the same pattern and generally contain the same key classes and concepts. The key classes are TestCase, TestRunner, TestFixture, TestSuite, and TestResult.

The architecture diagrams in this section leave out some methods and other design details for clarity and represent the generic xUnit design, not that of JUnit.

TestCase

xUnit's most elemental class is TestCase, the base class for a unit test. It is shown in Figure 3-1.

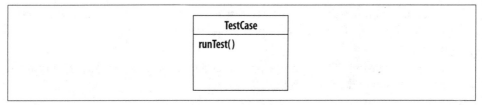

Figure 3-1. The abstract class TestCase, the parent of all xUnit unit tests

All unit tests are inherited from TestCase. To create a unit test, define a test class that is descended from TestCase and add a test method to it. Example 3-1 shows the unit test BookTest.

Example 3-1. BookTest, a test built on TestCase

BookTest.java
```java
import junit.framework.*;

public class BookTest extends TestCase {

   public void testConstructBook( ) {
      Book book = new Book("Dune");
      assertTrue( book.getTitle( ).equals("Dune") );
   }

}
```

The test method testConstructBook( ) uses assertTrue( ) to check the value of the Book's title. Test conditions always are evaluated by the framework's assert methods. If a condition evaluates to TRUE, the framework increments the successful test counter. If it is FALSE, a test failure has occurred and the framework records the details, including the failure's location in the code. After a failure, the framework skips the rest of the code in the test method, since the test result is already known.

BookTest tests the class Book, shown in Example 3-2.

Example 3-2. The class Book

Book.java
```java
public class Book {

    private String title = "";

    Book(String title) { this.title = title; }

    String getTitle( ) { return title; }
}
```

This is the Book class developed in Chapter 2, with a few changes. The title attribute is now private and the accessor function getTitle( ) is added.

BookTest can be run by adding a main( ) method that calls the test method, as shown in Example 3-3.

Example 3-3. BookTest with changes allowing it to be run

BookTest.java
```java
import junit.framework.*;

public class BookTest extends TestCase {

    public void testConstructBook( ) {
        Book book = new Book("Dune");
        assertTrue( book.getTitle( ).equals("Dune") );
    }

    public static void main(String args[]) {
        BookTest test = new BookTest( );
        test.testConstructBook( );
    }

}
```

Compiling and running BookTest produces a disappointing lack of output and not much confidence that anything actually happened.

```
> javac BookTest.java
> java BookTest
>
```

For the commands to work as shown, *junit.jar* and the directory containing the test classes must be in the Java classpath.

The results are more interesting if BookTest is made to fail by changing the assertTrue( ) condition to FALSE.

```
> java BookTest
Exception in thread "main" junit.framework.AssertionFailedError
    at junit.framework.Assert.fail(Assert.java:47)
    at junit.framework.Assert.assertTrue(Assert.java:20)
    at junit.framework.Assert.assertTrue(Assert.java:27)
    at BookTest.testConstructBook(BookTest.java:7)
    at BookTest.main(BookTest.java:12)
```

You can see that the unit test framework is doing its job, running the test and reporting the test failure. This demonstrates that an xUnit framework can be used in a very simple and straightforward way. Basic unit tests can be built on TestCase without any additional knowledge of the framework. However, the xUnits have other, more useful functionality to offer. One of the most valuable pieces is TestRunner.

TestRunner

A TestRunner reports details about the test results and simplifies the test. It is a fairly complex object that, in JUnit, comes in three flavors: the AWT TestRunner, the Swing TestRunner, and the textual TestRunner (cleverly named TextTestRunner.) Their purpose is to run one or more TestCases and report the results. Figure 3-2 shows TextTestRunner.

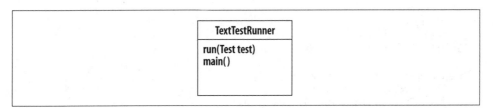

Figure 3-2. The class TextTestRunner

The important methods of TextTestRunner are run( ), which gives it a test to run, and main( ), which makes TextTestRunner a runnable class. TextTestRunner will be run with the test class BookTest as its argument. It will find the test method testConstructBook and run it.

You can remove the main( ) method in BookTest, since you no longer need it to run the test. Example 3-4 shows the refactored BookTest.

Example 3-4. BookTest made simple again

BookTest.java
```
import junit.framework.*;
```

Example 3-4. BookTest made simple again (continued)

```java
public class BookTest extends TestCase {

    public void testConstructBook( ) {
        Book book = new Book("Dune");
        assertTrue( book.getTitle( ).equals("Dune") );
    }

}
```

BookTest is reduced back to its essentials. Now, use TextTestRunner to run BookTest:

```
> java junit.textui.TestRunner BookTest
.
Time: 0.01

OK (1 test)
```

Using the TestRunner not only takes unnecessary code out of BookTest, but also provides a nice report of how many tests were run and how long they took.

Test classes often have multiple test methods. TestRunner will find all of the test methods that have names starting with test and run them. Example 3-5 shows BookTest with a second test method added. The new test validates a Book's author.

Example 3-5. BookTest with a second test method

BookTest.java
```java
import junit.framework.*;

public class BookTest extends TestCase {

    public void testConstructBook( ) {
        Book book = new Book("Dune", "");
        assertTrue( book.getTitle( ).equals("Dune") );
    }

    public void testAuthor( ) {
        Book book = new Book("Dune", "Frank Herbert");
        assertTrue( book.getAuthor( ).equals("Frank Herbert") );
    }

}
```

The author attribute and its accessor function getAuthor( ) are added to Book, as shown in Example 3-6.

Example 3-6. Book with an author attribute

Book.java
```java
public class Book {

    private String title = "";
```

Example 3-6. Book with an author attribute (continued)

```
    private String author = "";

    Book(String title, String author) {
        this.title = title;
        this.author = author;
    }

    public String getTitle() { return title; }
    public String getAuthor() { return author; }
}
```

Running BookTest shows that the framework now is running two tests:

```
> java junit.textui.TestRunner BookTest
..
Time: 0.01

OK (2 tests)
```

A dot is printed when each test is run as a progress indicator. The test output concludes with the number of tests and the elapsed time.

Most of the xUnits include a GUI TestRunner to provide enhanced visual feedback on the test results. The results are highlighted in green if all the tests succeed, or in red if there is a test failure. (This is the origin of the terms *green bar* and *red bar*. The TDD cycle is sometimes described as "Red-Green-Refactor" because of this. First, implement a new test that fails, causing a red bar; then, make the simplest possible code change that restores the green bar; finally, refactor the possibly ugly code that was introduced.) The chapters later in this book that describe specific versions of xUnit show screenshots of their TestRunner GUIs.

TestFixture

To explain test fixtures, another important xUnit concept, a more complex unit test example is useful. Functionality will be added to the Library class from Chapter 2 to allow multiple Books to be added and to get the number of Books the Library class contains. Example 3-7 gives an initial version of the unit test LibraryTest that tests these new features.

Example 3-7. Initial version of LibraryTest

```
LibraryTest.java
import junit.framework.*;
import java.util.*;

public class LibraryTest extends TestCase {

    public void testAddBooks() {
        Library library = new Library();
```

Example 3-7. Initial version of LibraryTest (continued)

```
        library.addBook(new Book("Dune", "Frank Herbert"));
        library.addBook(new Book("Solaris", "Stanislaw Lem"));
        Book book = library.getBook( "Dune" );
        assertTrue( book.getTitle().equals("Dune") );
        book = library.getBook( "Solaris" );
        assertTrue( book.getTitle().equals("Solaris") );
    }

    public void testLibrarySize() {
        Library library = new Library();
        library.addBook(new Book("Dune", "Frank Herbert"));
        library.addBook(new Book("Solaris", "Stanislaw Lem"));
        assertTrue( library.getNumBooks() == 2 );
    }

}
```

Two test methods are implemented. The method testAddBooks() adds two Books to the Library, then uses getBook() to verify that the additions succeeded. The method testLibrarySize() also adds two Books, then checks that getNumBooks() returns "2".

Example 3-8 shows the new version of Library with the additional functionality to pass the tests.

Example 3-8. New version of Library

Library.java
```java
import java.util.*;

public class Library {

    private Vector books;

    Library() {
        books = new Vector();
    }

    public void addBook( Book book ) {
        books.add( book );
    }

    public Book getBook( String title ) {
        for ( int i=0; i < books.size(); i++ ) {
            Book book = (Book) books.elementAt( i );
            if ( book.getTitle().equals(title) )
                return book;
        }
        return null;
    }

    public int getNumBooks() {
        return books.size();
```

Example 3-8. New version of Library (continued)

```
    }

}
```

Library now uses a Vector to contain a collection of Books. The new method getNumBooks( ) returns the number of Books in the collection. The methods addBook( ) and getBook( ) add and retrieve a Book from the collection.

When you use TextTestRunner to execute LibraryTest, both test methods succeed:

```
> java junit.textui.TestRunner LibraryTest
..
Time: 0.05

OK (2 tests)
```

LibraryTest has a number of problems. First and foremost, the amount of code duplication between the two test methods is bothersome. Both of them create a test Library and add two books to it. Second, another concern is what will happen if one of the asserts fails. The rest of the code in the test method will not be executed and any objects created will not be cleaned up. In Java, the garbage collector will deallocate objects automatically, but often unit tests use objects or resources that must be explicitly closed or deleted.

One way to take care of the code duplication is to make the test Library a member of LibraryTest and have the first test initialize it and add the initial two elements. The second test could assume that the first test succeeded, run its tests, and then clean up. Unfortunately, this solution introduces more potential problems. If the first test fails, the second also may fail because its initial conditions are wrong, even though there may be nothing wrong with the functionality it tests. The second test will always fail unless the first one is run before it, so they cannot be run separately or in reverse order. Furthermore, failure of either test is likely to result in things not getting cleaned up.

In general, well-written unit tests exhibit *isolation*. An isolated test doesn't depend in any way on the results of other tests. To ensure isolation, tests should not share objects that change. Tests that have interdependencies are *coupled*. In LibraryTest, if one of the test methods assumed that the other test left the Library in a certain state, it would be a classic example of test coupling.

The xUnit architecture helps to ensure test isolation with test fixtures. A test fixture is a test environment used by multiple tests. It is implemented as a TestCase with multiple test methods that share objects. The shared objects represent the common test environment. Figure 3-3 shows the relationship between a TestFixture and a TestCase.

Every TestCase is implicitly a TestFixture, although it may not act as one. The TestFixture behavior comes into play when multiple test methods have objects in

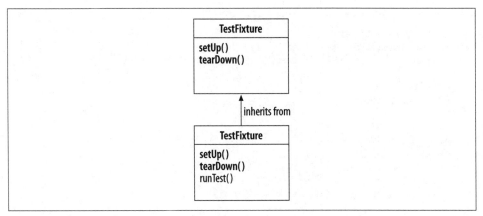

Figure 3-3. TestFixture and its child TestCase

common. The setUp( ) method is called prior to each test method, establishing the initial environment for the test. The tearDown( ) method is always called after each test method to clean up the test environment, even if there is a failure. Thus, although the tests use the same objects, they can make changes without the possibility of affecting the next test.

The TestFixture behavior effectively creates and destroys the test class each time one of its test methods is called. This may incur a performance penalty, but it is important to guarantee that the tests are isolated.

Incidentally, some xUnits (such as CppUnit) have an actual class or interface named TestFixture from which TestCase is descended, while some (JUnit) just allow TestCase to act as a TestFixture.

Writing tests as TestFixtures has a number of advantages. Test methods can share objects but still run in isolation. Test coupling is minimized. Test methods that share code can be grouped together in the same TestFixture. Code duplication between tests is reduced. The cleanup code is guaranteed to run whether a test succeeds or fails. Finally, the test methods can be run in any order, since they are isolated. Example 3-9 shows LibraryTest implemented as a TestFixture. In this example, the test fixture's shared environment contains an instance of Library with two Books.

Example 3-9. LibraryTest implemented as a TestFixture

LibraryTest.java
```
import junit.framework.*;
import java.util.*;

public class LibraryTest extends TestCase {

    private Library library;

    public void setUp() {
```

Example 3-9. LibraryTest implemented as a TestFixture (continued)

```
        library = new Library();
        library.addBook(new Book("Dune", "Frank Herbert"));
        library.addBook(new Book("Solaris", "Stanislaw Lem"));
    }

    public void tearDown() {
    }

    public void testGetBooks() {
        Book book = library.getBook( "Dune" );
        assertTrue( book.getTitle().equals( "Dune" ) );
        book = library.getBook( "Solaris" );
        assertTrue( book.getTitle().equals( "Solaris" ) );
    }

    public void testLibrarySize() {
        assertTrue( library.getNumBooks() == 2 );
    }

}
```

The stylistic improvements over the previous version of LibraryTest are apparent: the code duplication is gone, the test methods contain only statements specifically related to the test conditions, and the tests are easier to understand.

Note that the test method previously named testAddBooks() is renamed testGetBooks() to more accurately describe what it's doing.

When LibraryTest is run, the sequence of function calls is:

```
setUp()
testGetBooks()
tearDown()
setUp()
testLibrarySize()
tearDown()
```

The calls to setUp() and tearDown() initialize and deinitialize the test fixture each time a test method is called, thus isolating the tests.

TestSuite

So far, this review of xUnit has focused on writing single unit test classes, sometimes with multiple test methods. What about testing with multiple unit test classes? After all, each production object should have a corresponding unit test.

xUnit contains a class for aggregating unit tests called TestSuite. TestSuite is closely related to TestCase, since both are descendants of the same abstract class, Test. Figure 3-4 shows the Test interface and how TestSuite and TestCase implement it.

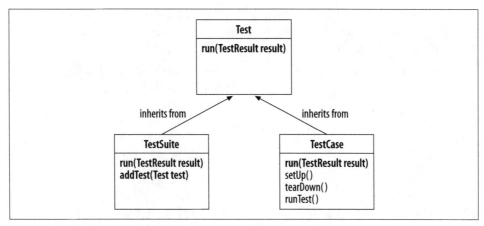

Figure 3-4. TestSuite, TestCase, and their parent interface Test

The interface Test contains the run( ) method that the framework uses to run tests and collect their results. Since TestSuite implements run( ), it can be run just like a TestCase. When a TestCase is run, its test methods are run. When a TestSuite is run, its TestCases are run. TestCases are added to a TestSuite using the addTest( ) method. Since a TestSuite is itself a Test, a TestSuite can contain other TestSuites, allowing the intrepid developer to build hierarchies of TestSuites and TestCases.

Example 3-10 shows a TestSuite-derived class named LibraryTests that contains both BookTest and LibraryTest.

Example 3-10. An instance of TestSuite named LibraryTests

LibraryTests.java
```java
import junit.framework.*;

public class LibraryTests extends TestSuite {

    public static Test suite( ) {
        TestSuite suite = new TestSuite( );
        suite.addTest(new TestSuite(BookTest.class));
        suite.addTest(new TestSuite(LibraryTest.class));
        return suite;
    }

}
```

A TestSuite is created for each of the test classes and added to LibraryTests. This is a quick way to add all of the test methods to the test suite at once. The addTest( ) method also may be used to add test methods to a test suite individually, as shown here:

```java
suite.addTest(new LibraryTest("testAddBooks"));
```

To be used this way, an instance of TestCase must have a constructor that takes a string argument and invokes its parent's constructor. The string argument specifies the name of the test method to run.

You can run instances of TestSuite using a TestRunner just as you would run a TestCase. The TestSuite's static method suite( ) is called to create the suite of tests to run.

```
> java junit.textui.TestRunner LibraryTests

....
Time: 0.06

OK (4 tests)
```

The results show that both of the test methods from the LibraryTest and BookTest unit test classes have been run, for a total of four tests.

TestResult

As shown in the discussion of the Test interface, TestResult is the parameter to Test's run( ) method. The immediate goal of running unit tests, in a literal sense, is to accumulate test results. The class TestResult serves this purpose. Each time a test is run, the TestResult object is passed in to collect the results. Figure 3-5 shows TestResult.

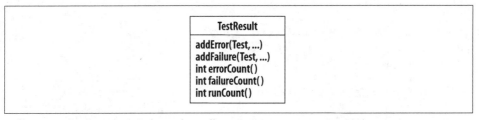

Figure 3-5. The class TestResult, used to collect test outcomes

TestResult is a simple object. It counts the tests run and collects test failures and errors so the framework can report them. The failures and errors include details about the location in the code where they occurred and any associated test descriptions. The information printed for the BookTest failure at the beginning of this chapter is typical.

xUnit Architecture Summary

The classes TestCase, TestRunner, TestFixture, TestSuite, and TestResult represent the core of the xUnit architecture. To understand what they do is to understand how xUnit works. Figure 3-6 shows how they all fit together.

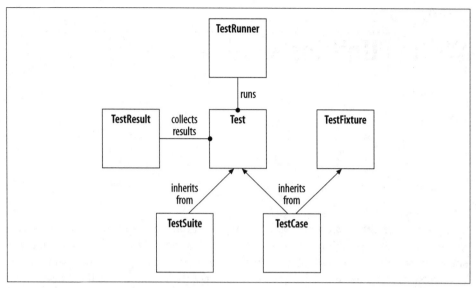

Figure 3-6. Core classes of the xUnit test framework architecture

The test classes created in this chapter and the classes they interact with are shown in Figure 3-7.

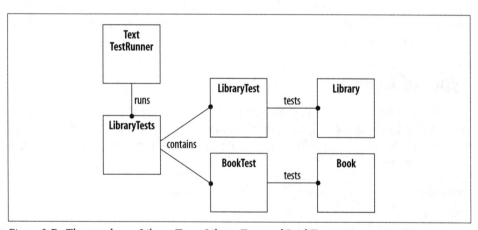

Figure 3-7. The test classes LibraryTests, LibraryTest, and BookTest

LibraryTests is a TestSuite containing BookTest and LibraryTest. LibraryTest is a TestFixture, and BookTest is a TestCase. Conceptually, TextTestRunner runs LibraryTests, which runs BookTest and LibraryTest, which in turn run their test methods.

This concludes the discussion of the generic xUnit architecture. Chapters 6 through 10 describe the specific architectural details of some popular versions of xUnit, with usage examples for each one.

CHAPTER 4
Writing Unit Tests

The previous chapters present a simple unit test framework and the fundamentals of xUnit. The unit test framework's architecture is important to understand, but not something you have to think about often. Most of your time should be spent writing unit tests, implementing production code to make the tests pass, or refactoring. This chapter includes examples of common patterns used when writing unit tests, as well as related tips on unit test development.

The code examples in this chapter are unit tests of additional virtual library functionality, including looking up books by author and title, looking up multiple books by one author, and removing books from the library. The Library and Book code to implement the new features is given at the end of the chapter.

Types of Asserts

The code examples shown so far use *plain asserts*. These are the most generic type of test assertion, which take a Boolean condition that must evaluate to TRUE for the test to succeed. A plain assert, the unit test for the Library method removeBook( ), is shown in Example 4-1.

Example 4-1. Test method testRemoveBook() using a plain assert

LibraryTest.java
```
public void testRemoveBook( ) {
    library.removeBook( "Dune" );
    Book book = library.getBook( "Dune" );
    assertTrue( book == null );
}
```

If the method removeBook( ) is stubbed out, the test fails. The following test results report the failure:

```
> java junit.textui.TestRunner LibraryTests
.....F.
Time: 0.06
```

```
There was 1 failure:
1) testRemoveBook(LibraryTest)junit.framework.AssertionFailedError
    at LibraryTest.testRemoveBook(LibraryTest.java:32)
    at sun.reflect.NativeMethodAccessorImpl.invoke0(Native Method)
    at sun.reflect.NativeMethodAccessorImpl.invoke(Unknown Source)
    at sun.reflect.DelegatingMethodAccessorImpl.invoke(Unknown Source)

FAILURES!!!
Tests run: 6,  Failures: 1,  Errors: 0
```

Although the line of code where the failure occurred is shown, the output does not describe the specific cause of the failure. It often is helpful to add an informative message to the assertion. The xUnits generally have two versions of every assert method, one of which takes a message parameter describing the assert. Example 4-2 shows the test method using an assert with a message.

Example 4-2. Test method using an assert with a message

LibraryTest.java
```
    public void testRemoveBook( ) {
        library.removeBook( "Dune" );
        Book book = library.getBook( "Dune" );
        assertTrue( "book is not removed", book == null );
    }
```

With the additional message, the rest results provide better information about the cause of the test failure:

```
1) testRemoveBook(LibraryTest)junit.framework.AssertionFailedError: book is not
removed
```

Although all assert conditions ultimately must evaluate to a Boolean result of TRUE or FALSE, it can be tedious to constantly reduce every expression to this form. The xUnits offer a variety of assert functions to help. Examples of several of the assert methods from JUnit are as follows:

```
assertFalse( book == null );
assertFalse( "book is null", book == null );
assertNull( book );
assertNull( "book is not null", book );
assertNotNull( book );
assertNotNull( "book is null", book );
assertEquals( "Solaris", book.title );
assertEquals( "unexpected book title", "Solaris", book.title );
```

These assert methods all have variants that take a message parameter to describe the failure, as shown above. The assertEquals( ) method has variants that take different data types as arguments.

Defining Custom Asserts

The basic assert methods cover only a few common cases. It's often useful to extend them to cover additional test conditions and data types. Custom assert methods save test coding effort and make the test code more readable.

So far, the Library tests check a Book's title attribute to verify the expected Book object, as shown in Example 4-3 in the test method testGetBooks( ).

Example 4-3. Test comparing two Books using their title attributes

LibraryTest.java

```
public void testGetBooks( ) {
    Book book = library.getBook( "Dune" );
    assertTrue( book.getTitle().equals( "Dune" ) );
    book = library.getBook( "Solaris" );
    assertTrue( book.getTitle().equals( "Solaris" ) );
}
```

To be really sure that the test Book is correct, the tests should also check the Book's author, but this means adding extra asserts to each test. It's clearly useful to have an assert method that compares an expected Book to the actual Book, checking all of the attributes. This new assert method is easy to implement by building on the generic assertTrue( ) method, as shown in Example 4-4.

Example 4-4. Custom assert method to compare Books

BookTest.java

```
public class BookTest extends TestCase {

    public static void assertEquals( Book expected, Book actual ) {
        assertTrue(expected.getTitle().equals( actual.getTitle() )
                && expected.getAuthor().equals( actual.getAuthor() ));
    }
}
```

The assert method assertEquals( ) takes expected and actual Book objects to compare. It succeeds if the title and author attributes of the two Books are equal. Example 4-5 shows how it is used.

Example 4-5. Using the custom assert method

LibraryTest.java
```
public class LibraryTest extends TestCase {

    private Library library;
    private Book book1, book2;

    public void setUp( ) {
        library = new Library( );
        book1 = new Book("Dune", "Frank Herbert");
```

Example 4-5. Using the custom assert method (continued)

```
    book2 = new Book("Solaris", "Stanislaw Lem");
    library.addBook( book1 );
    library.addBook( book2 );
  }

  public void testGetBooks( ) {
    Book book = library.getBook( "Dune" );
    BookTest.assertEquals( book1, book );
    book = library.getBook( "Solaris" );
    BookTest.assertEquals( book2, book );
  }
}
```

The custom assert method makes the test clear and concise and improves it by comparing all the Book attributes, not just the title. While writing tests, watch for complex assert conditions that are used repeatedly. They are good candidates for replacement with custom assert methods.

Single Condition Tests

A useful rule of thumb is that a test method should only contain a single test assertion. The idea is that a test method should only test one behavior; if there is more than one assert condition, multiple things are being tested. When there is more than one condition to test, then a test fixture should be set up, and each condition placed in a separate test method.

The xUnits tend to enforce this rule when handling test assertion failures. A test method returns as soon as a failure occurs, skipping any additional code. Running the rest of the test is unnecessary, since the result (failure) is known.

Practically speaking, test methods containing several assertions are not always a terrible thing. Tests may have conditions that can only be combined into one expression with unnecessary complication of the code. The testGetBooks( ) method in the previous section verifies that the Library contains two Books, which is most clearly expressed as two separate asserts, although they could be combined into one compound condition. A single behavior can have several side effects that you should check with separate assertions. So, it's not a problem when a test method contains several asserts, as long as the test method is only testing a single behavior.

However, a test method with many asserts is a clear indicator that a single test is doing too much. Example 4-6 shows a test method with this problem.

Example 4-6. Poorly written unit test that tests multiple behaviors

LibraryTest.java
```
  public void testLookupBooksByAuthor( ) {
    // Add two books by same author
    Book book3 = new Book( "Cosmos", "Carl Sagan" );
```

```
        Book book4 = new Book( "Contact", "Carl Sagan" );
        library.addBook( book3 );
        library.addBook( book4 );
        // Look up books by title and author
        Book book = library.getBook( "Cosmos", "Carl Sagan" );
        BookTest.assertEquals( book3, book );
        book = library.getBook( "Contact", "Carl Sagan" );
        BookTest.assertEquals( book4, book );
        // Look up both books by author
        Vector books = library.getBooks( "Carl Sagan" );
        assertEquals( "two books not found", 2, books.size() );
        book = (Book)books.elementAt(0);
        BookTest.assertEquals( book3, book );
        book = (Book)books.elementAt(1);
        BookTest.assertEquals( book4, book );
    }
```

How is this test flawed? Let us count the ways. It tests two separate behaviors: getting a Book by author and title and getting multiple Books by the same author. Looking up two books by two different methods means there are several results to test; thus, there are many asserts—five in all. Although it is sensible to check the results of all the operations, there are redundant tests, such as the two tests of the getBook( ) method. To get the test to pass, numerous changes must be made immediately to both Book and Library. The complexity of the changes increases the chance that a coding mistake will be made. When one assert in the sequence fails, the rest will be skipped, leaving it uncertain whether those asserts would succeed. So, if the Book lookup by title and author fails, it has to be fixed before the test that gets multiple Books is run. In other words, the tests are coupled so that failure of one may affect the success of the others.

When the number of asserts in a test method is excessive, change it into a test fixture with multiple test methods, each testing one behavior. In Example 4-7, refactoring the test method makes it apparent that the two lookup methods are distinct behaviors and should be tested separately.

Example 4-7. The previous test method refactored into separate test methods

LibraryTest.java
```
    public void setUp( ) {
        book3 = new Book( "Cosmos", "Carl Sagan" );
        book4 = new Book( "Contact", "Carl Sagan" );
        library.addBook( book3 );
        library.addBook( book4 );
    }

    public void testGetBookByTitleAndAuthor( ) {
        Book book = library.getBook( "Cosmos", "Carl Sagan" );
        BookTest.assertEquals( book3, book );
    }
```

Example 4-7. The previous test method refactored into separate test methods (continued)

```
public void testGetBooksByAuthor() {
    Vector books = library.getBooks( "Carl Sagan" );
    assertEquals( "two books not found", 2, books.size() );
    Book book = (Book)books.elementAt(0);
    BookTest.assertEquals( book3, book );
    book = (Book)books.elementAt(1);
    BookTest.assertEquals( book4, book );
}
```

Example 4-7 shows `LibraryTest` with the two separate test methods, one for each behavior. The code to add the two test `Books` is placed in the `setUp()` method. The tests are isolated and the code is simplified.

Testing Expected Errors

It is important to test the error-handling behavior of production code in addition to its normal behavior. Such tests generate an error and assert that the error is handled as expected. In other words, an expected error produces a unit test success.

The canonical example of a unit test that checks expected error handling is one that tests whether an expected exception is thrown, as shown in Example 4-8.

Example 4-8. Unit test for expected exception

LibraryTest.java
```
    public void testRemoveNonexistentBook() {
        try {
            library.removeBook( "Nonexistent" );
            fail( "Expected exception not thrown" );
        } catch (Exception e) {}
    }
```

The expected error behavior is that an exception is thrown when the `removeBook()` method is called for a nonexistent `Book`. If the exception is thrown, the unit test succeeds. If it is not thrown, `fail()` is called. The `fail()` method is another useful variation on the basic assert method. It is equivalent to `assertTrue(false)`, but it reads better.

Since the `removeBook()` method now throws an exception, the `testRemoveBook()` unit test should be updated, as shown in Example 4-9.

Example 4-9. Unit test that fails when an exception is thrown

LibraryTest.java
```
    public void testRemoveBook() {
        try {
            library.removeBook( "Dune" );
        } catch (Exception e) {
            fail( e.getMessage() );
```

```
        }
    Book book = library.getBook( "Dune" );
    assertNull( "book is not removed", book );
}
```

This example uses `fail( )` to cause the test to fail when an unexpected exception is thrown. The exception's message attribute is used as the assert message.

The same general pattern is followed to test expected error behavior that is not represented by an exception: the test fails if the error is not seen and succeeds if it is. Example 4-10 shows a unit test that attempts to get a nonexistent `Book` from the `Library` and asserts that the expected null `Book` is returned.

Example 4-10. Unit test checking the expected error getting a nonexistent Book

LibraryTest.java
```
    public void testGetNonexistentBook( ) {
        Book book = library.getBook( "Nonexistent" );
        assertNull( book );
    }
```

(Not) Testing Get/Set Methods

Every behavior should be covered by a unit test, but every method doesn't need its own unit test. Many developers don't test get and set methods, because a method that does nothing but get or set an attribute value is so simple that it is considered immune to failure. Tests of such methods are correspondingly trivial, as shown in the test of `getTitle( )` in Example 4-11.

Example 4-11. Trivial test of getTitle() method

BookTest.java
```
    public void testGetTitle( ) {
        Book book = new Book( "Solaris", "Stanislaw Lem" );
        assertEquals( "Solaris", book.getTitle( ) );
    }
```

If a get or set method produces any side effects or otherwise has nontrivial functionality, it should be tested. For example, with lazy initialization, a get method may compute an attribute value before returning it—behavior that deserves a unit test.

Testing Protected Behavior

A topic of much discussion within the unit testing community is how to test protected or private methods. Since access to such methods is restricted, writing unit tests for them is not straightforward.

Some developers deal with this quandary by simply ignoring protected or private methods and testing only the public interfaces. It's argued that most of an object's behavior is reflected in its public methods. The behavior of the protected methods can be inferred by the exposed behavior.

There are some drawbacks to this approach. If there are private methods that contain complex functionality, they will not be tested directly. There is a tendency to make everything public so that it is testable. Some behaviors that should be private might be exposed.

It is possible to access and test protected and private methods, depending on the specifics of how a language defines and enforces object access permissions. In C++, making the test class a `friend` of the production class allows it to access protected interfaces:

```
class Library {
#ifdef TEST
    friend class LibraryTest;
#endif
}
```

This introduces a reference to the test code into the production code, which is not good. Preprocessor directives such as `#ifdef TEST` can omit such references when the production code is built.

In Java, a simple technique that allows test classes to access protected and private methods is to declare the methods as package scope and place the test classes in the same package as the production classes. The next section, "Test Code Organization," shows how to arrange Java code this way.

For Java developers who are not satisfied with the direct approach, the Java Reflection API is a tricky way to overcome access protection. The JUnit extension "JUnit-addons" includes a class named `PrivateAccessor` that uses this approach to access protected or private attributes and methods.

The truly hardcore can follow the examples given here to write their own code that subverts access protection. In Example 4-12, the values of all of `Book`'s fields are read, regardless of protection. This approach is an ugly hack. Don't read this code just after a meal.

Example 4-12. Example showing use of Reflection API to get private field values

BookTest.java
```
import java.lang.reflect.*;

    public void testGetFields( ) {
        Book book = new Book( "test", "test" );
        Field fields[] = book.getClass( ).getDeclaredFields( );
        for ( int i = 0; i < fields.length; i++ ) {
            fields[i].setAccessible( true );
            try {
                String value = (String)fields[i].get( book );
```

Example 4-12. Example showing use of Reflection API to get private field values (continued)

```
            assertEquals( "test", value );
        } catch (Exception e) {
            fail( e.getMessage() );
        }
    }
}
```

A Book with title and author "test" is created. The Reflection API method getDeclaredFields() returns an array of all of the Book's fields, and the call to setAccessible() allows access to a field. The Reflection API method get() is used to obtain each field's value. The test asserts that the value of the field is test.

Similarly, in Example 4-13, all of Book's get methods are called, ignoring access protection (although the get methods actually are public).

Example 4-13. Example using Reflection API to invoke methods

BookTest.java
```
    public void testInvokeMethods() {
        Book book = new Book( "test", "test" );
        Method[] methods = book.getClass().getDeclaredMethods();
        for ( int i = 0; i < methods.length; i++ ) {
            if ( methods[i].getName().startsWith("get") ) {
                methods[i].setAccessible( true );
                try {
                    String value = (String)methods[i].invoke( book, null );
                    assertEquals( "test", value );
                } catch (Exception e) {
                    fail( e.getMessage() );
                }
            }
        }
    }
}
```

Paralleling the previous example, the Reflection API method getDeclaredMethods() returns all of the Book's methods, and the call to setAccessible() subverts the method's access protection. The test checks the method name and calls only those that have names starting with get to avoid calling Book's constructor. The Reflection API method invoke() is used to call the methods. Both get methods should return the value test, so this condition is asserted.

Hacks aside, the recommended approach is to design objects so that their important behaviors are public and test those behaviors. Structure the code so that the tests have access to the protected behaviors as well, so that they can be accessed if necessary.

Test Code Organization

As a project grows in size, organizing the files containing production and test code becomes an issue. Although keeping the test and production code in the same directory is the simplest solution, it is better to have a clean separation between the two categories of code. This strategy helps avoid build complications that occur when a directory contains some code that should be linked into the production application, and some that should not. Including the test code in the delivered application is undesirable because it unnecessarily increases the size of the delivery, and also because the tests may expose behavior or design details that the developer meant to keep "under the hood."

Organizing the code is a language-specific concern. In Java, the directory path to a source file parallels its package membership. The need to test protected interfaces means that unit tests should belong to the same package as the production classes they test, so they must have the same directory path. This can be done by creating separate but parallel hierarchies for the production and test code.

Figure 4-1 shows how the source code for the final version of the virtual library application is organized. There are three Java packages, `com.utf.library`, `com.utf.library.gui`, and `com.utf.library.xml`.

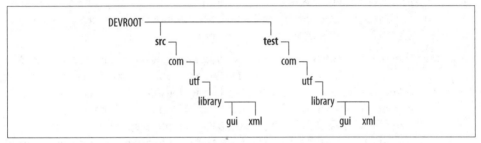

Figure 4-1. Organization of production and test code

The production and test code are located in separate directories, *src* and *test*, which are located under the project's top level *DEVROOT* directory. For example, the production class `Library` resides in the directory *src/com/utf/library*, and the test class `LibraryTest` is in *test/com/utf/library*. The test classes' package names parallel the production classes' package names, so the test classes can access and test protected behavior of the production code. Since the code is in separate directory trees, it is simple to build and run only the production or test code as desired.

For many other languages, an effective way to organize the code is to place all test code in a subdirectory named *test* within each production code directory. This arrangement keeps the test code separate, but makes linking it to the production code simple.

Mock Objects

Applications often use interfaces to external objects such as databases, web servers, network services, or hardware devices. Sometimes you must write and test code to interface with objects before they are actually available. Even when the external object is available in the development environment, using it in testing may involve lots of time-consuming, fragile set-up effort, such as loading test data, running services, or placing hardware in a known state. Mock objects are a way of dealing elegantly with this type of situation.

A *mock object* is a simulation of a real object. Mocks implement the interface of the real object and behave identically with it, to the extent necessary for testing. Mocks also validate that the code that uses them does so correctly. To pass the mock's validation, other objects must call the correct methods, with the expected parameters, in the expected order. A test object that simply stands in for a real object without providing such verification is not a mock; it is a stub.

Databases are commonly mocked objects. Code that interfaces to a database clearly is important to test. To be tested realistically, the code must be able to perform database operations such as opening and closing connections, reading and writing data, and performing transactions. However, running a live database in the development environment can be a pain. Tests often require that the database is in a specific state or that it contains a specific set of test data. If multiple developers run tests simultaneously, their database operations may interfere.

Mocking the database makes having an actual database unnecessary for testing. The mock has the same interface as the actual database object and the same behavior from the perspective of the client software, but it doesn't need to actually contain anything but a minimal implementation and possibly some test data. Once the database mock is created, it becomes much simpler to write tests that assume that the database is in various states. Testing becomes faster and easier without the overhead of interfacing with an actual database engine.

To illustrate this, let's create a mock object representing a database connection object. An interface called DBConnection represents a database connection, as shown in Example 4-14.

Example 4-14. The interface DBConnection, representing a database connection

DBConnection.java
```
public interface DBConnection {
    void connect();
    void close();
    Book selectBook( String title, String author );
}
```

The class LibraryDB retrieves Books from a database using DBConnection. It is shown in Example 4-15.

Example 4-15. The database interface LibraryDB

LibraryDB.java
```
public class LibraryDB {
```

Example 4-15. The database interface LibraryDB (continued)

```java
    private DBConnection connection;

    public LibraryDB( DBConnection c ) {
        connection = c;
    }

    Book getBook( String title, String author ) {
        connection.connect( );
        Book book = connection.selectBook( title, author );
        connection.close( );
        return book;
    }
}
```

We would like to build a unit test for LibraryDB, but we don't have an actual database yet. So, we'll mock DBConnection as shown in Example 4-16.

Example 4-16. The mock object MockDBConnection

MockDBConnection.java
```java
public class MockDBConnection implements DBConnection {

    private boolean connected = false;
    private boolean closed = false;

    public void connect( ) { connected = true; }
    public void close( ) { closed = true; }
    public Book selectBook( String title, String author ) {
        return null;
    }

    public boolean validate( ) {
        return connected && closed;
    }

}
```

MockDBConnection implements the public interface of DBConnection, so it can be used in the interface's place. MockDBConnection uses the attributes connected and closed to record that the connect( ) and close( ) methods have been called. The validate( ) method verifies the connection's state by checking these flags. So, the expectation set by the mock is that code using DBConnection must call both connect( ) and close( ).

The test class LibraryDBTest is shown in Example 4-17.

Example 4-17. The test class LibraryDBTest

LibraryDBTest.java
```java
import junit.framework.*;
import java.util.*;

public class LibraryDBTest extends TestCase {
```

Example 4-17. The test class LibraryDBTest (continued)

```
public void testGetBook( ) {
    MockDBConnection mock = new MockDBConnection( );
    LibraryDB db = new LibraryDB( mock );
    Book book = db.getBook( "Cosmos", "Carl Sagan" );
    assertTrue( mock.validate( ) );
}
}
```

The test method `testGetBook( )` creates an instance of `MockDBConnection`, uses it to construct a `LibraryDB`, and then calls the `LibraryDB` method `getBook( )`. The success of the test depends on the result of the mock's `validate( )` function. If the mock is in the expected state, its validation succeeds and the test passes. The mock object verifies the expected sequence of calls to the database connection and validates that `LibraryDB` is interacting with it correctly. It also allows `LibraryDB` and `DBConnection` to be tested without an actual database.

More sophisticated mock objects go beyond simply setting flags for each method called by recording the arguments provided for method calls, the order of calls, and other details of the method's state. In this way, mock objects can perform sophisticated validation of interobject interactions.

Mock objects are a deep topic, covered by numerous web sites, books, and online groups. Also, a variety of tools are available to support mock object development for various domains and languages, including EasyMock, jMock, and MockRunner.

AbstractTest

Just like regular classes, abstract classes and interfaces should have their own unit tests. Designing such tests is not straightforward, because these object types cannot be directly instantiated. We'd also like to ensure that every descendant of an abstract class passes the parent object's tests. The AbstractTest pattern is the answer.

An AbstractTest is itself abstract, like the tested object. It contains an abstract factory method, which produces an instance of the object to test. It also contains the test methods for the abstract class. They resemble ordinary unit test methods, but test instances of the abstract class created by the factory method.

To test a concrete class that is descended from the abstract class, the unit test is subclassed from the AbstractTest. Its factory method returns an instance of the concrete class. When the concrete unit test is run, the AbstractTest is run as well. So, the AbstractTest tests every concrete implementation of the abstract class.

Let's create an AbstractTest for the interface `DBConnection`. We'll add the method `isOpen( )` to it, as shown in Example 4-18.

Example 4-18. The interface DBConnection

DBConnection.java
```java
public interface DBConnection {
    void connect();
    void close();
    boolean isOpen();
    Book selectBook( String title, String author );
}
```

The AbstractTest should test the behavior of the interface to make sure that any concrete implementation of it is correct. Tests of the isOpen( ) method should verify that it returns TRUE after connect( ) is called, and FALSE after close( ) is called. The AbstractTest class AbstractDBConnectionTestCase, shown in Example 4-19, provides these tests.

Example 4-19. The AbstractTest class AbstractDBConnectionTestCase

AbstractDBConnectionTestCase.java
```java
import junit.framework.*;

public abstract class AbstractDBConnectionTestCase extends TestCase {

    public abstract DBConnection getConnection();

    public void testIsOpen() {
        DBConnection connection = getConnection();
        connection.connect();
        assertTrue( connection.isOpen() );
    }

    public void testClose() {
        DBConnection connection = getConnection();
        connection.connect();
        connection.close();
        assertTrue( !connection.isOpen() );
    }
}
```

The AbstractTest specifies a factory method, getConnection( ). Concrete tests that descend from it will implement the factory method, allowing the test methods testIsOpen( ) and testClose( ) to test an instance of the concrete class. Notice how these methods use getConnection( ) to get the DBConnection to test.

AbstractTests have names ending in "TestCase," which is different from other test classes. A separate naming convention for AbstractTest classes makes them easily recognizable. Some unit test tools assume that any class named ending with "Test" are test classes that should be instantiated and run, and the different naming convention avoids confusion.

To see the AbstractTest run, we need to define a concrete class descended from DBConnection and a corresponding concrete unit test descended from

AbstractDBConnectionTestCase. The concrete class JDBCConnection is shown in Example 4-20.

Example 4-20. The concrete class JDBCConnection

JDBCConnection.java

```java
public class JDBCConnection implements DBConnection {

    private String connectString;
    private boolean open;

    public JDBCConnection( String connect ) {
        connectString = connect;
        open = false;
    }

    public void connect() { open = true; }
    public void close() { open = false; }
    public boolean isOpen() { return open; }
    public String getConnectString() { return connectString; }
    public Book selectBook( String title, String author ) {
        return null;
    }
}
```

JDBCConnection is an initial version of an interface to a JDBC database engine. It differs from the base DBConnection by its member connectString, which contains the URL of a JDBC database connection.

The unit test JDBCConnectionTest tests JDBCConnection. It is derived from the AbstractTest. It is shown in Example 4-21.

Example 4-21. The concrete test JDBCConnectionTest

JDBCConnectionTest.java

```java
public class JDBCConnectionTest extends AbstractDBConnectionTestCase {

    public DBConnection getConnection() {
        return new JDBCConnection( "jdbc:odbc:testdb" );
    }

    public void testConnectString() {
        JDBCConnection connection = (JDBCConnection)getConnection();
        String connStr = connection.getConnectString();
        assertTrue( connStr.equals("jdbc:odbc:testdb") );
    }
}
```

JDBCConnectionTest implements the factory method getConnection( ) and one test method, testConnectString( ). When the test is instantiated and run, the two test methods in the parent AbstractTest also will be run to test instances of JDBCConnection. This way, the AbstractTest verifies that the concrete subclass passes the tests of the parent interface.

Performance Tests

Like the mock object, unit testing for performance is its own significant topic. Software performance often is neglected at the unit testing level, and is only taken into consideration during functional testing. However, performance-oriented unit tests are powerful tools, especially for applications that require specific performance goals be met. It's been reported that Apple's Safari browser was developed in an environment that automatically ran performance tests on any code that was checked in. The code was rejected if it did not meet or exceed the speed standards of previous versions. Thus, the unit tests ensured that the code's performance is continuously improving.

When a piece of code has a performance problem, it is very useful to first write a test that reveals the problem. This performance test not only lets you know when the code has achieved the desired performance, but also acts as a "canary in the coal mine" that indicates if the performance degrades again.

Tools intended specifically for performance-oriented unit testing are available, such as JUnitPerf. However, it is not difficult to develop performance tests within any unit test framework. This section gives an example of a unit test that tests the speed of retrieving a Book from a Library.

The initial question when writing a performance test is this: what is the performance criterion that the test must meet to pass? Usually, this is expressed in terms of the amount of time that a certain action may take. If the action takes too long, the criterion has not been met, and the test fails.

The Library class developed so far has a very poorly performing algorithm to get a Book. It serially reads through the collection of Books, doing string comparisons on each one until the desired Book is found. This awful lookup stratagem is ideal for demonstrating a performance test that fails initially, but succeeds after a little refactoring. Example 4-22 shows the unit test class LibraryPerfTest.

Example 4-22. Performance unit test LibraryPerfTest

LibraryPerfTest.java
```
import junit.framework.*;
import java.util.*;

public class LibraryPerfTest extends TestCase {

    private Library library;

    public void setUp() {
        library = new Library();
        for ( int i=0; i < 100000; i++ ) {
            String title = "book" + i;
            String author = "author" + i;
            library.addBook(new Book( title, author ));
```

Example 4-22. Performance unit test LibraryPerfTest (continued)

```
        }
    }

    public void testGetBookPerf( ) {
        double maxTime = 100; // milliseconds
        long startTime = System.currentTimeMillis( );
        Book book = library.getBook( "book99999" );
        long endTime = System.currentTimeMillis( );
        long time = endTime-startTime;
        assertTrue( time < maxTime );
        assertEquals( "book99999", book.getTitle( ) );
    }
}
```

LibraryPerfTest is implemented as a test fixture since it is likely that more performance tests will be implemented. The setUp( ) method adds 100,000 Books to the Library. The test method testGetBookPerf( ) tests the amount of time it takes to look up a Book. It uses the method currentTimeMillis( ) to get the system time before and after the getBook( ) operation, calculates the elapsed time, and compares it to a performance criterion of 100 milliseconds (0.1 second). As a sanity check, it also asserts that the expected Book was found.

With the Vector-based implementation of Library, the unit test fails:

```
> java -classpath ".;junit.jar" junit.textui.TestRunner LibraryPerfTest
.F
Time: 0.562
There was 1 failure:
1) testGetBookPerf(LibraryPerfTest)junit.framework.AssertionFailedError
        at LibraryPerfTest.testGetBookPerf(LibraryPerfTest.java:23)
        at sun.reflect.NativeMethodAccessorImpl.invoke0(Native Method)
        at sun.reflect.NativeMethodAccessorImpl.invoke(Unknown Source)
        at sun.reflect.DelegatingMethodAccessorImpl.invoke(Unknown Source)

FAILURES!!!
Tests run: 1,  Failures: 1,  Errors: 0
```

Library can be refactored to use a Hashtable to store Books. (The refactored Library code is given in the next section, "New Library and Book Code.") With this change, lookups by title are efficient, and the test passes:

```
> java -classpath ".;junit.jar" junit.textui.TestRunner LibraryPerfTest
.
Time: 0.734

OK (1 test)
```

The total test time has increased. This is because addBook( ) takes longer to add a Book with the Hashtable implementation.

The hardcoded time value of 100 milliseconds used in this example can produce different results when the test is run on faster or slower platforms. Even when run on the same platform, varying machine loads and process priorities mean that a performance test can succeed or fail on subsequent runs without any code changes. Accounting for such variations can present a challenge when designing performance tests. There are a number of techniques to deal with these problems. Consistently running performance tests on the same platform is helpful. Test timing can be based on the time required to run a reference operation rather than on a hardcoded time value, allowing for system performance variations. Timing multiple repetitions of an operation reduces the effect of transient glitches. Finally, performance tests can use order-of-magnitude timing ranges rather than exact minimum timings, so that code meeting general performance goals will pass.

New Library and Book Code

Example 4-23 gives the code for the version of Book referenced in this chapter.

Example 4-23. The class Book

Book.java

```java
public class Book {

    private String title = "";
    private String author = "";

    Book(String title, String author) {
        this.title = title;
        this.author = author;
    }

    public String getTitle() { return title; }
    public String getAuthor() { return author; }

}
```

The code for the final version of Library is given in Example 4-24. It uses a Hashtable to store the collection of Books.

Example 4-24. The class Library

Library.java

```java
import java.util.*;

public class Library {

    private Hashtable books;

    Library() {
        books = new Hashtable();
    }
```

Example 4-24. The class Library (continued)

```java
    public void addBook( Book book ) {
        books.put( book.getTitle( ), book );
    }

    public Book getBook( String title ) {
        return (Book)books.get( title );
    }

    public Book getBook( String title, String author ) {
        return (Book)books.get( title );
    }

    public Vector getBooks( String author ) {
        Vector auth_books = new Vector( );
        for ( Enumeration e = books.elements(); e.hasMoreElements( ); ) {
            Book book = (Book)e.nextElement( );
            if ( book.getAuthor( ).equals(author) )
                auth_books.add( book );
        }
        return auth_books;
    }

    public void removeBook( String title ) throws Exception {
        if ( books.remove( title ) == null )
            throw new Exception("Book not found");
    }

    public int getNumBooks( ) {
        return books.size( );
    }

    public void empty( ) {
        books.clear( );
    }

}
```

CHAPTER 5

Unit Testing GUI Applications

Unit tests for ordinary software objects are easy to conceptualize. Objects have behaviors that are represented by methods and attributes. Tests elicit these behaviors to validate them. Unit testing of GUI objects is a different and more complex problem.

GUI objects are the graphical elements that make up the user interface of most software applications. They include windows, buttons, frames, text boxes, menus, and many other types of widgets. Even very simple applications often contain dozens of them. GUI objects usually have many behaviors, such as responding to mouse movements or clicks, displaying values, being shown, hidden, highlighted, disabled, and so forth. You usually build GUI applications from standard toolkits, such as Java's Swing, wxWindows for C++, or .NET's WinForms. Most of the GUI object behavior is provided, and you simply assemble the standard objects and write code only to implement the custom behaviors of their application.

Doing test-first development of such GUI code is challenging. It may not be hard to test the process of simply creating and displaying an object, such as a window. As soon as it becomes necessary to test responses to user actions such as keyboard entries or mouse clicks, the tests can become very complicated. It often takes a good deal of messy code to create and test a single GUI element as a standalone unit. Sometimes it is not even possible to design an automated test that verifies a specific visual GUI behavior, such as "the dialog box pops up modally showing the alert icon and the warning message in red." The test has no way of validating how a dialog would appear to a user. In general, trying to test application logic by simulating user interaction with the GUI is labor-intensive and error-prone.

Consider the pseudocode shown in Example 5-1, which represents a typical event-handling method in a class implementing a dialog window. The code responds to a mouse click on a button by getting values from the dialog's text fields, validating them, calculating a result, and updating a document. If the validation fails, an error dialog is shown. In either case, the text fields are cleared and the dialog is redrawn.

Example 5-1. A typical dialog event handler method

```
void handleEvent( ) {
   switch ( eventType ) {
      case ( buttonClick ) :
         getTextFieldValues( );
         if ( validateValues( ) ) {
            calculateResult( );
            updateDocument( );
         } else { // validation failed
            showErrorDialog( );
         }
         clearTextFields( );
         redraw( );
   }
}
```

How should this dialog be unit tested? Each step in the event handler is a behavior that deserves its own unit test. The overall result of clicking on the button should be tested, as well as the error case when bad values are entered and a message dialog appears. Testing this will require complex GUI event scripting. For each behavior tested, the tests may have to create the dialog window, fill in text field values, fire a mouse click event, verify that the resulting window state is as expected, and close the dialog. The tests could be affected by unexpected events, such as someone clicking on the dialog while it is being tested.

So, how can GUI objects be tested effectively, in a way that supports test driven development? One answer is laid out in an influential paper about this problem: "The Humble Dialog Box" by Michael Feathers. It points out that building GUIs using the standard tools usually leads to GUI objects that contain all the application logic pertaining to their functionality. Such objects are hard to work with in the context of a test harness, and the contained application logic is hard to separate from the GUI behavior for testing. The way to solve this problem is by creating *smart objects* that are not themselves GUI objects, but that contain the functional behavior relevant to a particular GUI object. These smart objects can be easily unit tested like any other class. Once a smart object is in place, a thin GUI view object called a *humble dialog* can be created that knows how to display the smart object's information, but that contains no application logic or complex behavior. As much as possible, the humble dialog contains only GUI objects with standard behavior, as well as get/set methods that simply read or write values for the GUI elements to display. Testing the GUI behavior then becomes largely optional. If it is tested, these tests don't need to address the functional behavior contained in the smart object.

With the humble dialog approach, the design of GUI object code tends to resemble that shown in Figure 5-1.

These classes will implement an "Add Book" dialog for creating a Book. It will be a simple dialog containing a title field, an author field, and Add and Cancel buttons, as shown in Figure 5-2. The smart object AddBook is where all the functional behavior is

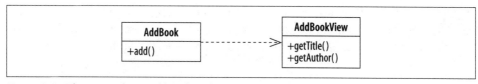

Figure 5-1. The smart object AddBook and its view class AddBookView

located. For each behavior, there is a method—in this case, add( ). The view class AddBookView is a thin object containing the actual GUI objects, such as the window frame, text fields, and buttons. The only custom code it contains is methods to get the field values. Thus, testing the smart object's functionality does not require creating and interacting with the GUI, and testing the view involves only tests of GUI behavior, not application logic.

Figure 5-2. GUI design sketch for the AddBook dialog window

Splitting GUI applications into a presentation layer and a business layer that contains all of the logic is an approach that has long been popular. It makes perfect sense for client-server and web-based applications, where the data and the view are on separate machines. The document-view model follows this philosophy as well, in which all the data lives in a document object and all the presentation-related code is contained in view objects. The humble dialog approach differs from these older architectural ideas by emphasizing that all the important functionality must reside in the smart object. The view object should not contain any functional state, data validation, or other nontrivial logic. This way, all of the functionality can be validated without having to perform complex and fragile GUI testing.

Library GUI

This chapter presents a Java Swing implementation of a GUI for the virtual library. It demonstrates test driven development of a GUI application and serves as a more realistic example of a working library application than the previous chapters. However, it is still a demonstration program rather than a practically useful application.

The functional goal of the library GUI is to allow a user to add new Books to a Library and look up existing Books. Nothing fancy, but like most GUI applications, there are many elements and behaviors to consider. The application will need a main window, dialogs for adding and finding Books, and standard GUI functionality such as being able to open and close windows.

Adhering to the TDD mantra, first identify a behavior and write a test for it. The initial target is the Add Book dialog described earlier, which provides a GUI interface for creating a new Book. Example 5-2 shows the unit test for the smart object AddBook.

Example 5-2. Initial unit test for the smart object AddBook

AddBookTest.java
```
public class AddBookTest extends TestCase {

    public void testAddBook() {
        Library library = new Library();
        AddBook addBook = new AddBook(library);
        addBook.add("The Dragons of Eden", "Carl Sagan");
        assertNotNull( library.getBooksByTitle("The Dragons of Eden") );
    }
}
```

This test creates an AddBook object, calls its method add( ), and verifies that the Book has been added to the Library. AddBook's constructor gives the test the Library to modify; this was an up-front design decision.

The initial implementation of AddBook to pass AddBookTest is shown in Example 5-3.

Example 5-3. Initial version of the smart object AddBook

AddBook.java
```
public class AddBook {

    private Library library;

    public AddBook(Library lib) {
        library = lib;
    }

    public void add(String title, String author) {
        Book book = new Book( title, author );
        try {
            library.addBook( book );
        } catch (Exception e) {}
    }
}
```

Since the method addBook( ) may throw an exception, add( ) must catch it. Informing the user about the error is something to add to the "to-do" list. Otherwise, the implementation is simple.

The next step is to create the view class, AddBookView. It needs to provide a GUI window, text fields for the title and author, and Add and Cancel buttons. The window title should be "Add Book." The unit test AddBookViewTest verifies all of this, as shown in Example 5-4.

Example 5-4. The unit test AddBookViewTest

AddBookViewTest.java
```java
public class AddBookViewTest extends TestCase {

    public void testControlValues() {
        AddBookView view = new AddBookView();
        assertEquals( "Add Book", view.getTitle() );
        assertEquals( "", view.titleField.getText() );
        assertEquals( "", view.authorField.getText() );
        assertEquals( "Add", view.addButton.getText() );
        assertEquals( "Cancel", view.cancelButton.getText() );
    }
}
```

Example 5-5 gives the initial implementation of AddBookView. It is a custom subclass of the Swing GUI class JFrame and contains only the minimum code necessary to pass the test. It completely ignores the layout of the controls.

Example 5-5. The initial version of AddBookView

AddBookView.java
```java
import java.awt.*;
import javax.swing.*;

public class AddBookView extends JFrame {

    protected JTextField titleField;
    protected JTextField authorField;
    protected JButton cancelButton;
    protected JButton addButton;

    public AddBookView() {
        super("Add Book");

        Container contentPane = this.getContentPane();

        // Add labels and text fields
        JLabel label1 = new JLabel("Title", Label.RIGHT);
        contentPane.add(label1);
        titleField = new JTextField("", 60);
        contentPane.add(titleField);
        JLabel label2 = new JLabel("Author", Label.RIGHT);
        contentPane.add(label2);
        authorField = new JTextField("", 60);
        contentPane.add(authorField);
        // Add buttons
        cancelButton = new JButton("Cancel");
        contentPane.add(cancelButton);
        addButton = new JButton("Add");
        contentPane.add(addButton);
    }
}
```

When Java creates a JFrame-derived dialog window, it does not display it until its show( ) method is called. So, the test AddBookViewTest creates, verifies, and destroys the AddBookView dialog without actually showing it.

Now AddBook can be made to use AddBookView. Some thought must be given to how the smart object and the humble dialog will interact. They will communicate via an implicit internal protocol. The ideal architecture will place all the important behavior in the smart object, and will place all the GUI-related code, such as event handling, in the view. Having both the smart object and the view know about each other is unnecessary. The only necessary interaction between the two is that the view needs to be able to call the methods on the smart object representing its behaviors, so we will follow that model. When the view is constructed, it will get a reference to its smart object.

The most important functionality of this construct is to add a Book when the user clicks on the Add button in the view. This is a GUI-driven behavior, so the unit test belongs in AddBookViewTest. It also implicitly tests that the view invokes the smart object's add( ) method. Example 5-6 shows this test.

Example 5-6. AddBookViewTest with test of the Add button

AddBookViewTest.java
```java
public class AddBookViewTest extends TestCase {

    private Library library;
    private AddBook addBook;
    private AddBookView view;

    public void setUp() {
        library = new Library();
        addBook = new AddBook(library);
        view = new AddBookView(addBook);
    }

    public void testAddButton() {
        view.titleField.setText("The Dragons of Eden");
        view.authorField.setText("Carl Sagan");
        view.addButton.doClick();
        assertEquals(1,
            library.getBooksByTitle("The Dragons of Eden").size());
    }
}
```

AddBookViewTest is refactored as a test fixture that creates instances of Library, AddBook, and AddBookView in its setUp( ) method. The new test method, testAddButton( ), sets the title and author text field values, simulates a user click on the Add button using the method JButton.doClick( ), and verifies that the Book is added to the Library.

To pass this test, AddBookView requires a number of additions, including a reference to an AddBook and the ability to handle the button click event. Example 5-7 shows the new version of AddBookView. The code to create and add the controls is moved to a new method, addControls( ) (which is not shown, for brevity).

Example 5-7. AddBookView with "Add" button functionality

AddBookView.java
```java
public class AddBookView extends JFrame
      implements ActionListener {

   protected JTextField titleField;
   protected JTextField authorField;
   protected JButton cancelButton;
   protected JButton addButton;
   private AddBook addBook;

   public AddBookView(AddBook ab) {
      super("Add Book");
      addBook = ab;
      addControls( );
      addButton.addActionListener( this );
      cancelButton.addActionListener( this );
   }

   public void actionPerformed(ActionEvent e) {
      String cmd = e.getActionCommand( );
      System.out.println(cmd);
      if ( cmd.equals("Add") ) {
         addBook.add(titleField.getText(), authorField.getText( ));
      }
      else
         System.out.println("cmd not handled: "+cmd);
   }
}
```

The result of the changes to AddBookView is that it receives notification of user events via the actionPerformed( ) method. If the event indicates that the Add button was clicked, it calls the method AddBook.add( ) with the title and author values.

Now the Add Book dialog can be tried out manually. Example 5-8 shows a simple executable class called CreateAddBook that creates the dialog.

Example 5-8. Simple executable class to create AddBook dialog

CreateAddBook.java
```java
public class CreateAddBook {

   public static void main(String[] args) {
      CreateAddBook create = new CreateAddBook( );
   }

   public CreateAddBook( ) {
```

Example 5-8. Simple executable class to create AddBook dialog (continued)

```
        Library library = new Library( );
        AddBook addBook = new AddBook(library);
        AddBookView view = new AddBookView(addBook);
        view.show( );
        while (view.isVisible( )) {}
        System.exit(0);
    }
}
```

Assuming that the directory containing the library classes is in the Java CLASSPATH, CreateAddBook is run as follows:

```
    $ java CreateAddBook
```

The Add Book dialog appears as just a titlebar. It can be resized to show that the Add button fills the entire frame, as shown in Figure 5-3.

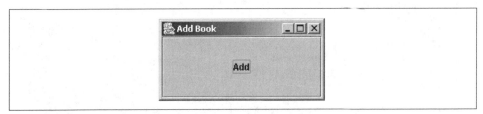

Figure 5-3. The AddBook dialog as it initially appears

The dialog is effectively useless because nothing is being done in AddBookView to arrange and size the controls. Once a better layout is implemented, the dialog looks much better, as shown in Figure 5-4.

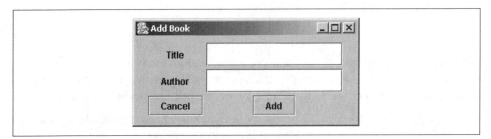

Figure 5-4. The AddBook dialog with improved layout

Example 5-9 shows the method addControls( ) with the new layout code. Aside from arranging the controls with a GridBagLayout, the method sets the dialog to a usable default size with the setSize( ) method.

Example 5-9. addControls() with improved layout code

AddBookView.java
```
    protected void addControls( ) {
        Container contentPane = this.getContentPane( );
```

Example 5-9. addControls() with improved layout code (continued)

```
    contentPane.setLayout(new GridBagLayout( ));
    GridBagConstraints c = new GridBagConstraints( );

    // Add labels and text fields
    JLabel label1 = new JLabel("Title", Label.RIGHT);
    c.insets = new Insets(2, 2, 2, 2);
    c.gridx = 0;
    c.gridy = 0;
    contentPane.add(label1, c);
    titleField = new JTextField("", 60);
    titleField.setMinimumSize(new Dimension(180, 30));
    c.gridx = 1;
    contentPane.add(titleField, c);
    JLabel label2 = new JLabel("Author", Label.RIGHT);
    c.gridx = 0;
    c.gridy = 1;
    contentPane.add(label2, c);
    authorField = new JTextField("", 60);
    authorField.setMinimumSize(new Dimension(180, 30));
    c.gridx = 1;
    contentPane.add(authorField, c);
    // Add buttons
    cancelButton = new JButton("Cancel");
    c.gridx = 0;
    c.gridy = 2;
    contentPane.add(cancelButton, c);
    addButton = new JButton("Add");
    c.gridx = 1;
    contentPane.add(addButton, c);

    setSize(300, 140);
  }
```

Why isn't there a unit test for the new layout code? It is overkill to write unit tests for purely visual attributes such as layout positions and control sizes. Not only are such tests tedious to write, but their value is limited. If someone adjusts the position of a control, the code's functional behavior does not change, so why should the unit test fail?

Now a working Add Book dialog is in place, along with unit tests of its functionality. The library GUI needs a lot more to be usable, including a main window, a Find Book dialog, and a lot of related GUI functionality and application logic. Rather than walking through all the steps to build this application, this description skips ahead to the finished result. The final version of the library GUI application contains a number of GUI elements implemented as smart objects with thin view classes, including:

- AddBook and AddBookView

- FindBookByTitle and FindBookByTitleView

- LibraryFrame and LibraryFrameView

The class `LibraryFrame` is the main application window with an attached menu bar. It acts as the parent for the other windows. Closing it causes the application to exit. It is shown in Figure 5-5.

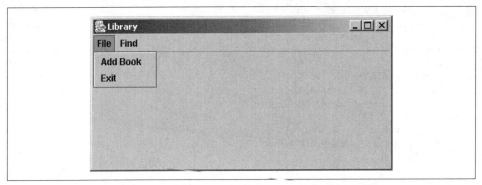

Figure 5-5. The LibraryFrame window

Since the view classes have duplicate code and the same interface, it makes sense to create a common base class. The abstract parent class `BaseView` is a simple subclass of `JFrame`. Example 5-10 shows the code for `BaseView`.

Example 5-10. The abstract base class BaseView

BaseView.java
```
public abstract class BaseView extends JFrame
     implements ActionListener {

   BaseView(String title, int width, int height) {
      super(title);
      addControls();
      setSize(width, height);
   }

   public abstract void actionPerformed(ActionEvent e);
   protected abstract void addControls();
}
```

BaseView gives the view classes a consistent interface and eliminates code duplication between them. As an abstract class, BaseView should be tested with an AbstractTest. BaseViewTestCase is shown in Example 5-11.

Example 5-11. The AbstractTest BaseViewTestCase

BaseViewTestCase.java
```
public abstract class BaseViewTestCase extends TestCase {

   public abstract BaseView getBaseView();

   public void testNotVisible() {
      BaseView view = getBaseView();
```

Example 5-11. The AbstractTest BaseViewTestCase (continued)

```
      assertFalse( view.isVisible( ) );
   }

   public void testShow( ) {
      BaseView view = getBaseView( );
      view.show( );
      assertTrue( view.isVisible( ) );
   }

   public void testClose( ) {
      BaseView view = getBaseView( );
      view.show( );
      WindowEvent e = new WindowEvent(view,
         WindowEvent.WINDOW_CLOSING);
      Toolkit.getDefaultToolkit().getSystemEventQueue( ).postEvent(e);
      try {
         Thread.currentThread( ).sleep(100);
      } catch(Exception x) {}
      assertFalse( view.isVisible( ) );
   }
}
```

The AbstractTest tests three behaviors that all classes derived from `BaseView` should exhibit: they are hidden upon creation, become visible after the `show( )` method is called, and are hidden again after a `WINDOW_CLOSING` event is sent.

The unit tests for the view classes derived from `BaseView` should be subclasses of `BaseViewTestCase`. Example 5-12 shows `AddBookViewTest` implemented this way.

Example 5-12. AddBookViewTest implemented as a subclass of BaseViewTestCase

AddBookViewTest.java
```
public class AddBookViewTest extends BaseViewTestCase {

   private Library library;
   private AddBook addBook;
   private AddBookView view;

   public BaseView getBaseView( ) {
      return new AddBookView( addBook );
   }

   public void setUp( ) {
      library = new Library( );
      addBook = new AddBook( library );
      view = (AddBookView)getBaseView( );
      view.show( );
   }

   public void tearDown( ) {
      addBook = null;
      library = null;
```

```
    }

    public void testAddButton( ) {
        view.titleField.setText("The Dragons of Eden");
        view.authorField.setText("Carl Sagan");
        view.addButton.doClick( );
        assertEquals(1, library.getBooksByTitle("The Dragons of Eden").size( ));
        assertEquals( "", view.titleField.getText( ) );
        assertEquals( "", view.authorField.getText( ) );
        assertFalse( view.isVisible( ) );
    }
}
```

Note how the test implements and uses the factory method getBaseView( ) to create an instance of AddBookView for the tests.

In conclusion, although unit tests for a GUI-driven application use different strategies than tests for ordinary classes, the same basic patterns of unit test development are followed. Each class has a corresponding test class, and each behavior is tested with a separate test method.

CHAPTER 6

JUnit

Overview

The JUnit unit test framework is the reference implementation of xUnit. As its name implies, it is developed in and used with Java. It is undoubtedly the most widely used, extended, and discussed framework for software unit testing today. JUnit is the foundation for more specialized unit testing tools, including Cactus, Jester, JUnit-Perf, and many more, and integrates closely with others, such as Ant. The large community of JUnit users means that it is the basis for many new ideas and developments in unit testing technology.

The generic xUnit architecture, described in Chapter 3, reflects the architecture of JUnit. Java is designed from the ground up as a true object-oriented language, incorporating many modern features such as pure abstract classes, object reflection, and native exception-handling. JUnit makes full use of these features.

The purpose of JUnit is to provide a framework for building and running unit tests. The JUnit distribution also is a great example of a simple, solid software product that is built using test driven development. Examining its source code is instructive.

JUnit is open source software released under the Common Public License. This license frees all contributors from any liability or responsibility for the code, and makes users free to distribute, copy, alter, sell, and otherwise have their way with it. For details, refer to *http://www.opensource.org*.

The definitive source for everything pertaining to JUnit is *http://www.junit.org*. The information given in this book is based on JUnit 3.8.1, the current version of JUnit as of this writing.

Architecture

JUnit contains about 75 named classes plus a number of inner classes and interfaces. It is organized into packages, as shown in Figure 6-1.

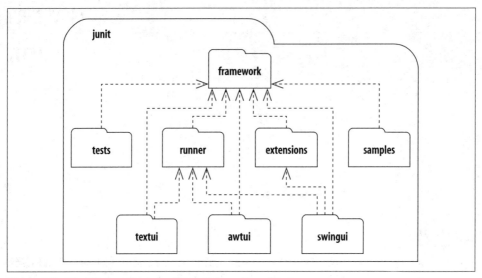

Figure 6-1. The JUnit packages and their import dependencies

The package junit.framework represents the core functionality, and the foundation on which unit tests are built. Much of the rest of the code is the relatively complex Swing, AWT, and text user interface (UI) packages, the package junit.samples (containing unit test examples), and the package junit.tests (containing JUnit's own unit tests). JUnit's developers "eat their own dog food" by providing a complete set of unit tests for all of its functionality.

The class architecture for the package junit.framework is shown in Figure 6-2.

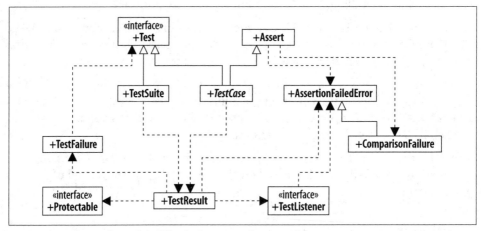

Figure 6-2. Class architecture of the package junit.framework

The architecture of junit.framework follows the generic xUnit architectural model described in Chapter 3. In particular, notice a key architectural element, the interface

Test, which is implemented by the classes TestCase and TestSuite. The abstract class TestCase is the parent of all unit test classes.

As described in Chapter 3, the key classes used when building unit tests are TestCase, TestSuite, and the TestRunners. Appendix B is a detailed class reference for the junit.framework package.

Usage

This section presents a quick overview of basic JUnit usage. The xUnit examples in the previous chapters provide a more detailed review of how to use JUnit.

Test classes in JUnit are subclasses of TestCase. Tests can be built in a number of ways, but the conventional approach is described here. The name of the test class starts with the name of the object being tested and ends with Test. Test classes contain a separate test method for each behavior being tested. Test methods are named starting with test.

Test conditions are checked with *test assert methods*. Test asserts result in test success or failure. If the assert fails, the test method returns immediately. If it succeeds, the execution of the test method continues. Since a test method should only test a single behavior, in most cases, each test method should only contain one test assert.

If there are objects that are shared by the test methods, they should be initialized in the setUp( ) method and destroyed in tearDown( ). These methods are called before and after each test method call, effectively recreating the test fixture for each test, thereby providing test isolation.

Example 6-1 shows a test class built following this model, called LibraryTest, that (naturally) tests the class Library.

Example 6-1. The test class LibraryTest

LibraryTest.java
```java
import junit.framework.*;
import java.util.*;

public class LibraryTest extends TestCase {

    private Library library;

    public void setUp( ) throws Exception {
        library = new Library( );
        library.addBook(new Book( "Cosmos", "Carl Sagan" ));
        library.addBook(new Book( "Contact", "Carl Sagan" ));
        library.addBook(new Book( "Solaris", "Stanislaw Lem" ));
        library.addBook(new Book( "American Beauty", "Allen M Steele" ));
        library.addBook(new Book( "American Beauty", "Edna Ferber" ));
    }
```

Example 6-1. The test class LibraryTest (continued)

```
   public void tearDown( ) {
      library.empty( );
      library = null;
   }

   public void testGetBooksByTitle( ) {
      Vector books = library.getBooksByTitle( "American Beauty" );
      assertEquals( "wrong number of books found", 2, books.size( ) );
   }

   public void testGetBooksByAuthor( ) {
      Vector books = library.getBooksByAuthor( "Carl Sagan" );
      assertEquals( "2 books not found", 2, books.size( ) );
   }

   public void testEmpty( ) {
      library.empty( );
      assertEquals( "library not empty", 0, library.getNumBooks( ) );
   }
}
```

LibraryTest is a test fixture because there are multiple test methods sharing an object—in this case, an instance of Library. The Library is created and loaded with a set of Books in setUp( ) and emptied and disposed of in tearDown( ).

Each test method verifies a distinct behavior of the Library class with a single test assert. Although the tests may modify the Library, as shown by testEmpty( ), the test fixture functionality guarantees that each test runs in a clean fixture, without dependencies on the results of the others.

Tests are run using one of the TestRunner tools provided with JUnit. The simplest and most easily automated of these is TextTestRunner. Example 6-2 demonstrates using TextTestRunner to run LibraryTest.

Example 6-2. Running LibraryTest with the TextTestRunner

```
$ java junit.textui.TestRunner LibraryTest
.........
Time: 0.01

OK (3 tests)
```

It often is useful to aggregate multiple tests so they can be run together. The class TestSuite is used to contain a collection of tests. Example 6-3 shows a class, LibraryTests, which creates a TestSuite containing a number of test classes. The static method suite( ) creates and returns the TestSuite.

Example 6-3. The class LibraryTests

LibraryTests.java
```
import junit.framework.*;
```

Example 6-3. The class LibraryTests (continued)

```
public class LibraryTests extends TestSuite {

    public static Test suite( ) {
        TestSuite suite = new TestSuite( );
        suite.addTest(new TestSuite(BookTest.class));
        suite.addTest(new TestSuite(LibraryTest.class));
        suite.addTest(new TestSuite(LibraryDBTest.class));
        suite.addTest(new TestSuite(LibraryPerfTest.class));
        return suite;
    }
}
```

When LibraryTests is run using TextTestRunner, all of the test methods in each test class are found and run, as shown in Example 6-4.

Example 6-4. Running the LibraryTests test suite

```
$ java junit.textui.TestRunner LibraryTests
.................
Time: 0.851

OK (17 tests)
```

The GUI TestRunner can be used instead of TextTestRunner. The Swing version of TestRunner is invoked for LibraryTest as shown:

```
$ java junit.swingui.TestRunner LibraryTest
```

Figure 6-3 shows the result after the TestRunner GUI runs LibraryTest.

Test Assert Methods

A range of test assert methods are provided by JUnit. They are implemented as public static methods of the class Assert, which is a parent class of TestCase. Thus, every test class inherits these methods.

The most generic test assert method is assertTrue( ), which simply passes or fails based on the value of a Boolean argument. The other test assert methods are specialized versions of assertTrue( ) that handle particular types of test conditions. For example, the following test assert statements are equivalent:

```
assertTrue( book.title.equals("Cosmos") );
assertEquals( "Cosmos", book.title );
```

These statements are equivalent as well:

```
assertTrue( false )
fail( )
```

The specialized test assert methods are useful because they save coding effort, are easier to read, and allow more specific reporting of the results.

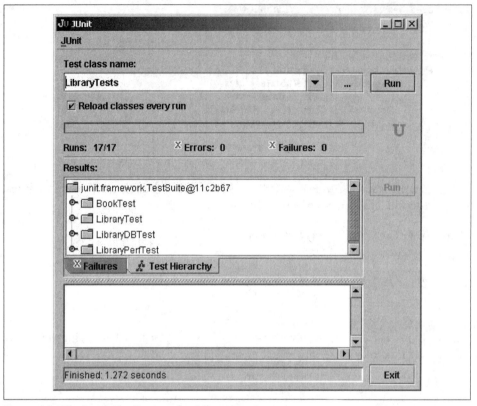

Figure 6-3. The Swing TestRunner after LibraryTest is run

The assert methods all have two variants, one that takes a String message as the first argument, and one that doesn't. The message allow you to provide a more detailed description of an assertion failure.

The assertEquals( ) methods compare the values of two arguments. They assume that the first value is the correct or "expected" value to which the second "actual" value should be compared. These methods will work if the arguments are reversed, but the failure message will be misleading.

The JUnit assert methods are described in the following list:

```
static void assertTrue(boolean condition)
static void assertTrue(message, boolean condition)
```
    The assertTrue assertion passes if condition is true. This is the most generic type of assertion.

```
static void assertFalse(boolean condition)
static void assertFalse(message, boolean condition)
```
    Test passes if condition is false.

```
static void assertEquals(expected, actual)
static void assertEquals(message, expected, actual)
```
Test passes if expected and actual are equal. Versions of this method exist to compare arguments of type boolean, byte, char, int, long, Object, short, or String.

```
static void assertEquals(expected, actual, delta)
static void assertEquals(message, expected, actual, delta)
```
Asserts equality of two values within a tolerance of delta. A delta of 0.0 tests exact equality. Versions of this method exist to handle arguments of type double or float.

```
static void assertNotNull(Object object)
static void assertNotNull(message, Object object)
```
Test passes if Object is not null.

```
static void assertNull(Object object)
static void assertNull(message, Object object)
```
Test passes if Object is null.

```
static void assertNotSame(Object expected, Object actual)
static void assertNotSame(message, Object expected, Object actual)
```
Test passes if the two Objects are not the same Object, as determined by the == operator.

```
static void assertSame(Object expected, Object actual)
static void assertSame(message, Object expected, Object actual)
```
Test passes if the two Objects are the same Object, as determined by the == operator.

```
static void fail( )
static void fail(message)
```
Test that always fails. It is equivalent to assertTrue(false).

CHAPTER 7

CppUnit

Overview

CppUnit is a port of JUnit to C++, and was originally authored by Michael Feathers and Jerome Lacoste. Its basic architecture and usage closely follow the xUnit model. The implementation details differ from JUnit as a result of design choices by CppUnit's developers and language differences between Java and C++. CppUnit's implementation makes full use of advanced C++ language features, including templates, abstract classes, nested classes, and the Standard Template Library (STL) It also makes extensive use of C macros, which some consider inelegant and error-prone, but are definitely useful here. CppUnit is designed to be thread-safe.

CppUnit is open source software released under the GNU Lesser General Public License. This license makes the code free for use, modification, and redistribution. For details, refer to *http://www.gnu.org*.

The CppUnit project is based at *http://cppunit.sourceforge.net*. The information given here is for CppUnit Version 1.8.0.

Architecture

CppUnit contains 24 ordinary classes, 4 abstract classes, 7 template classes, and several nested classes and helper macros. Everything belongs to the namespace "CppUnit" or one of its subordinate namespaces. The CppUnit namespaces are shown in Figure 7-1.

Most of the code belongs to the main namespace, "CppUnit." The namespace "Asserter" contains assertion functions used in test assert macros. "TestAssert" contains the function template assertEquals( ) and the method assertDoubleEquals( ). The "Ui" namespaces contain text, MFC, and QT versions of TestRunner.

Just as in JUnit, CppUnit's central design element is an abstract interface called Test implemented by classes named TestCase and TestSuite, as shown in Figure 7-2.

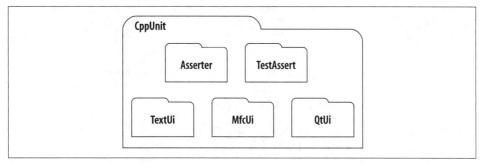

Figure 7-1. The CppUnit namespaces

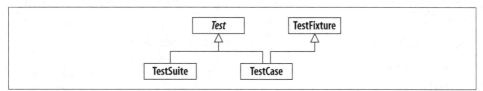

Figure 7-2. The key Test classes

TestCase represents an actual test object, and TestSuite is a composite of other Test objects. The class TestFixture represents the test fixture interface implemented by TestCase, with setUp( ) and tearDown( ) methods.

The object architecture for collecting test results is more complex than in JUnit. The key classes pertaining to test result handling are shown in Figure 7-3.

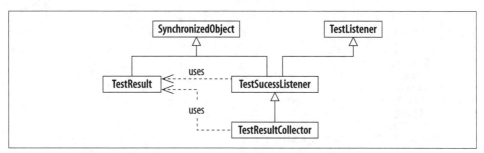

Figure 7-3. Classes to collect test results

The class TestResult receives test results as Test objects are run. However, it does not store the results but instead uses the TestListener interface to inform observers of test results. The TestListener subclass TestResultCollector stores the test results for reporting. As shown in Figure 7-3, these classes are derived from Synchronized-Object. This allows their operations to be mutex-protected so that tests and listeners may execute safely in separate, concurrent threads.

Output of test results is handled by classes implementing the Outputter interface, shown in Figure 7-4.

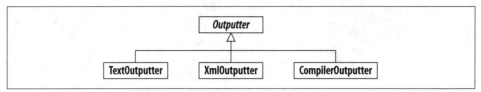

Figure 7-4. The Outputter classes for printing test results

The Outputter objects print the test results in human-readable text format, as an XML document, or in an IDE-compatible ("compiler") format.

The class TestRunner provides a convenient interface for running tests. CppUnit includes a generic text TestRunner as well as GUI versions of TestRunner for use in Qt and MFC development environments.

Appendix C is a class reference giving the low-level design details of CppUnit.

Usage

When writing unit tests using CppUnit, the general xUnit model is followed, as described in Chapters 3 and 6. Test objects are derived from TestCase and are run using a TestRunner. A number of code examples are given here to illustrate details of its usage. The examples are unit tests of a simple class named Book, shown in Example 7-1.

Example 7-1. The class Book

Book.h
```
using std::string;

class Book {

 public:
   Book( string const &title )
     : m_title( title ) {}

   string getTitle() { return m_title; }

 private:
   string m_title;

};
```

The simplest way to write a CppUnit unit test is to derive a class from TestCase and override its runTest( ) method. An example of such a unit test is given in Example 7-2.

Example 7-2. The simple test class BookTest

BookTest.h
```
#include "cppunit/TestCase.h"
#include "Book.h"

using std::string;

class BookTest : public CppUnit::TestCase {

 public:
   BookTest( string const &name ) : CppUnit::TestCase( name ) {}

   void runTest() {
      Book book( "Cosmos" );
      CPPUNIT_ASSERT( book.getTitle() == "Cosmos" );
   }

};
```

The test method runTest( ) creates a Book and uses the test assertion macro CPPUNIT_ASSERT( ) to test the title value. The test class is run by calling runTest( ). The simple program in Example 7-3 illustrates this.

Example 7-3. A simple program to run the test class BookTest

test.cpp
```
#include <iostream>
#include "BookTest.h"

int main( ) {
   try {
      BookTest test( "BookTest" );
      test.runTest();
      std::cout << "SUCCESS!" << std::endl;
      return 0;
   } catch ( ... ) {
      std::cout << "FAILURE!\n" << std::endl;
      return 1;
   }
}
```

If runTest( ) throws an exception, the failure is reported. Here, the test succeeds:

```
> ./test
SUCCESS!
```

The test can be made to fail by changing the title test value:

```
CPPUNIT_ASSERT( book.getTitle() == "Moscow" );
```

The output reports the failure:

```
> ./test
FAILURE!
```

The program test returns an error code of 1 in case of failure, which can be useful if an automated test script runs it.

This basic approach to writing unit tests is cumbersome. A new test class is implemented for each test method, and the runTest( ) method for each one must be called directly. The test results are reported only in a very simple way, as overall success or failure, with no details about what was tested and what failed.

The next step in increasing the sophistication of CppUnit test development is to implement unit tests as test fixtures, which allows multiple test methods to be implemented in one test class. Running them using a TestRunner provides nice reporting of the results.

An author attribute is added to Book in Example 7-4.

Example 7-4. Book with an author attribute

Book.h
```
using std::string;

class Book {

  public:
    Book(string const &title, string const &author)
      : m_title( title ), m_author( author ) {}

    string getTitle() { return m_title; }
    string getAuthor() { return m_author; }

  private:
    string m_title;
    string m_author;
};
```

BookTest can have two test methods, one testing each attribute of Book. Since both test methods can test the same Book, it makes sense to implement BookTest as a fixture. Example 7-5 shows the new version of BookTest.

Example 7-5. BookTest written as a test fixture with two test methods

BookTest.h
```
#include "cppunit/TestCase.h"
#include "Book.h"

using std::string;

class BookTest : public CppUnit::TestFixture {

  private:
    Book *book;

  public:
```

Example 7-5. BookTest written as a test fixture with two test methods (continued)

```cpp
    void setUp() {
        book = new Book( "Cosmos", "Carl Sagan" );
    }

    void tearDown() {
        delete book;
    }

    void testTitle() {
        CPPUNIT_ASSERT_EQUAL( string("Cosmos"), book->getTitle() );
    }

    void testAuthor() {
        CPPUNIT_ASSERT_EQUAL( string("Carl Sagan"), book->getAuthor() );
    }

};
```

The fixture contains a test Book, which is created in setUp( ) and deleted in tearDown( ). The two test methods are named testTitle( ) and testAuthor( ). It is conventional to give test methods a name starting with "test".

The test assertion macro CPPUNIT_ASSERT_EQUAL( ) is used to test the value of the title and author attributes. This macro handles arguments of many common data types, including std::string, as shown in Example 7-5.

The test program can use the text TestRunner to run BookTest, as shown in Example 7-6.

Example 7-6. Using the text TestRunner to run BookTest

test.cpp
```cpp
#include "cppunit/ui/text/TestRunner.h"
#include "cppunit/TestCaller.h"
#include "BookTest.h"

int main() {
    CppUnit::TextUi::TestRunner runner;
    runner.addTest( new CppUnit::TestCaller<BookTest>(
                    "testTitle",
                    &BookTest::testTitle ) );
    runner.addTest( new CppUnit::TestCaller<BookTest>(
                    "testAuthor",
                    &BookTest::testAuthor ) );
    if ( runner.run() )
        return 0;
    else
        return 1;
}
```

A TestCaller is created for each test method and added to the TestRunner using its addTest( ) method. The TestRunner runs each test method as a separate test—setting up and tearing down the fixture each time—and then reports the test results:

```
> ./test
..

OK (2 tests)
```

A failure can be produced in testAuthor( ) by changing the test condition:

```
CPPUNIT_ASSERT_EQUAL( string("Anonymous"), book->getAuthor( ) );
```

The details of the failure are reported, including the test name and source code location for the assertion that failed:

```
> ./test
..F

!!!FAILURES!!!
Test Results:
Run:  2   Failures: 1   Errors: 0


1) test: testAuthor (F) line: 25 BookTest.h
expected: Anonymous
but was:  Carl Sagan
```

As multiple text fixtures are developed, they can be added to a TestSuite, which aggregates them and makes running them a one-step operation. Example 7-7 demonstrates creating a TestSuite. The static method suite( ) is added to BookTest to return its suite of tests.

Example 7-7. Creating a TestSuite for BookTest's test methods

BookTest.h
```
static CppUnit::Test *suite( )
{
    CppUnit::TestSuite *suite
        = new CppUnit::TestSuite( "BookTest" );
    suite->addTest( new CppUnit::TestCaller<BookTest>(
                    "testTitle",
                    &BookTest::testTitle ) );
    suite->addTest( new CppUnit::TestCaller<BookTest>(
                    "testAuthor",
                    &BookTest::testAuthor ) );
    return suite;
}
```

The code to run the tests is simplified when they are run as a suite, as shown in Example 7-8.

Example 7-8. Running the test suite with the TestRunner

test.cpp
```
#include "cppunit/ui/text/TestRunner.h"
#include "cppunit/TestCaller.h"
#include "BookTest.h"

int main( ) {
   CppUnit::TextUi::TestRunner runner;
   runner.addTest( BookTest::suite( ) );
   if ( runner.run( ) )
      return 0;
   else
      return 1;
}
```

CppUnit includes helper macros that eliminate some of the coding effort by automatically creating TestSuite objects. The static method suite( ) in BookTest can be replaced by a series of macro calls, as shown in Example 7-9.

Example 7-9. Using helper macros to replace the suite() method

BookTest.h
```
   CPPUNIT_TEST_SUITE( BookTest );
   CPPUNIT_TEST( testTitle );
   CPPUNIT_TEST( testAuthor );
   CPPUNIT_TEST_SUITE_END( );
```

The macro call CPPUNIT_TEST_SUITE( ) creates the static method suite( ) to return a TestSuite. The CPPUNIT_TEST( ) calls add the two test methods to the suite. The call CPPUNIT_TEST_SUITE_END( ) is necessary to end the declaration of the suite.

The macro CPPUNIT_TEST_EXCEPTION( ) adds a test method that is expected to throw an exception to the test suite. The test passes if the expected exception is thrown. To demonstrate this, the constructor for Book is modified to throw an std::exception if the title is empty. Example 7-10 shows the new test method for this behavior, testInvalidTitle( ), and shows how it is added to the test suite.

Example 7-10. Using CPPUNIT_TEST_EXCEPTION to add an expected exception test

BookTest.h
```
   void testInvalidTitle( ) throw (std::exception) {
      Book *badBook = new Book( "", "Mark Twain" );
   }

   CPPUNIT_TEST_SUITE( BookTest );
   CPPUNIT_TEST( testTitle );
   CPPUNIT_TEST( testAuthor );
   CPPUNIT_TEST_EXCEPTION( testInvalidTitle, std::exception );
   CPPUNIT_TEST_SUITE_END( );
```

Example 7-11 shows the Book constructor modified to throw an std::exception.

Example 7-11. Book constructor modified to throw exception

Book.h
```
Book(string const &title, string const &author)
  : m_title( title ), m_author( author )
{
  if ( m_title.empty() )
     throw std::exception();
}
```

When run, testInvalidTest() creates a Book with an empty title, the constructor throws the expected exception, and the test passes.

The similar macro CPPUNIT_TEST_FAILURE() adds a test that is expected to fail to the test suite, as shown in Example 7-12.

Example 7-12. Adding an expected failure test to the test suite

BookTest.h
```
void testAlwaysFails() {
   CPPUNIT_FAIL( "Expected failure" );
}

CPPUNIT_TEST_SUITE( BookTest );
CPPUNIT_TEST_FAIL( testAlwaysFails );
CPPUNIT_TEST_SUITE_END();
```

Another useful helper macro is CPPUNIT_TEST_SUITE_REGISTRATION(). It is used to register test suites with the TestFactoryRegistry, as shown in Example 7-13.

Example 7-13. Registering a test suite and using the registry to create a test

test.cpp
```
#include "cppunit/ui/text/TestRunner.h"
#include "cppunit/TestCaller.h"
#include "BookTest.h"

int main() {

  CPPUNIT_TEST_SUITE_REGISTRATION( BookTest );

  CppUnit::TextUi::TestRunner runner;
  CppUnit::TestFactoryRegistry &registry
     = CppUnit::TestFactoryRegistry::getRegistry();
  runner.addTest( registry.makeTest() );
  if ( runner.run() )
     return 0;
  else
     return 1;
}
```

The registry automatically creates a TestSuite containing all of the registered tests. The call registry.makeTest() returns the TestSuite to run. This feature is

---

particularly useful when there are many tests and writing the code to add them all to a TestSuite would be tedious.

The related helper macro CPPUNIT_TEST_SUITE_NAMED_REGISTRATION( ) is used to add TestSuite objects to a named registry. The named registry is used to create a TestSuite containing its set of registered tests. This allows tests to be divided into groups that may be run separately.

Test Assert Methods

CppUnit provides several variations on the basic assert method. The assert methods are implemented as macros. The advantage of using macros to implement assert methods is that they enable the compiler preprocessor to record the source code location of each assert, which is otherwise hard to do in C.

As in other xUnits, some of the asserts have variants that take a descriptive message argument. The message is reported if the test fails. Examples of these variants are shown in the following list:

CPPUNIT_ASSERT(condition)
CPPUNIT_ASSERT_MESSAGE(message,condition)
> Test that passes if condition is true.

CPPUNIT_FAIL(message)
> Test that always fails.

CPPUNIT_ASSERT_EQUAL(expected,actual)
CPPUNIT_ASSERT_EQUAL_MESSAGE(message,expected,actual)
> Test that passes if expected and actual are equal. It supports arguments of most common data types and std::string.

CPPUNIT_ASSERT_DOUBLES_EQUAL(expected,actual,delta)
> Test that passes if expected and actual are equal within a tolerance of delta. The arguments are of type double.

CHAPTER 8

NUnit

Overview

NUnit is a unit test framework for the Microsoft .NET architecture. Conceptually, it follows the xUnit model, serving as a foundation for building unit test classes and methods. It is implemented in C#, but supports writing unit tests in any .NET language, including C#, J#, Managed C++, and Microsoft Visual Basic .NET (VB.NET). NUnit defines tests using C# attributes rather than object inheritance, so the details of its software architecture differ significantly from JUnit.

NUnit is open source software released under a public license. The license permits NUnit to be freely redistributed and altered, as long as the original copyright notice is included and any alterations are acknowledged. The copyright holders and main developers of NUnit are James Newkirk, Michael Two, Alexei Vorontsov, Philip Craig, and Charlie Poole.

For additional information refer to the NUnit web site, *http://www.nunit.org*. The summary in this chapter is based on Version 2.1.

Architecture

NUnit is a full-featured unit test framework built using TDD. The distribution includes unit tests covering all of NUnit's functionality. Aside from the core framework, NUnit also includes GUI and console test runners, code samples, extensions, and utilities.

NUnit relies on C# attributes to structure test code. In contrast to the conventional object-oriented definition of an attribute, a C# attribute is metadata attached to a code element such as a class or method. These attributes contain descriptive declarations that may be accessed at runtime. NUnit attributes such as Test and TestFixture allow the test framework to identify test methods and classes. This approach makes it possible to build unit tests with minimal knowledge of the underlying NUnit code structure.

Usage

A test class is defined using the TestFixture attribute. Test methods are defined using the Test attribute. Example 8-1 shows a simple unit test for the class Book. The source code for the classes Book and Library is given at the end of this section.

Example 8-1. The test class BookTest

BookTest.cs
```
using System;

namespace LibraryTests
{
    using Library;
    using NUnit.Framework;

    [TestFixture]
    public class BookTest
    {
        [Test]
        public void TestCreateBook( )
        {
            Book book = new Book( "Cosmos", "Carl Sagan" );
            Assert.AreEqual( "Cosmos", book.title, "wrong title" );
            Assert.AreEqual( "Carl Sagan", book.author, "wrong author" );
        }
    }

}
```

In this example, the test class BookTest is defined as a TestFixture, and the method TestCreateBook( ) is a Test. At runtime, all of the Test methods are found and run.

The attributes SetUp and TearDown are used to implement test fixture behavior. The SetUp method is called prior to each Test method, and the TearDown method is called afterwards. Example 8-2 shows a test for the class Library, implemented as a test fixture.

Example 8-2. The test class LibraryTest

LibraryTest.cs
```
using System;

namespace LibraryTests
{
    using Library;
    using NUnit.Framework;
```

Example 8-2. The test class LibraryTest (continued)

```csharp
[TestFixture]
public class LibraryTest
{
    private Library library;

    [SetUp]
    public void SetUp( )
    {
        library = new Library( );
        library.addBook(new Book( "Cosmos", "Carl Sagan" ));
        library.addBook(new Book( "Contact", "Carl Sagan" ));
    }

    [TearDown]
    public void TearDown( )
    {
    }

    [Test]
    public void TestGetBookByTitleAndAuthor( )
    {
        Book book = library.getBook( "Cosmos", "Carl Sagan" );
        Assert.AreEqual( "Cosmos", book.title, "wrong title" );
        Assert.AreEqual( "Carl Sagan", book.author, "wrong author" );
    }

    [Test]
    public void TestRemoveBook( )
    {
        library.removeBook( "Cosmos" );
        Book book = library.getBook( "Cosmos", "Carl Sagan" );
        Assert.IsNull( book, "book not removed" );
    }
}
```

The SetUp( ) method creates a Library and adds two Books to it. Since C# has automatic garbage collection, it is not necessary for the TearDown( ) method to deallocate the test objects.

Like other xUnits, NUnit provides numerous test assert methods. Examples 8-1 and 8-2 demonstrate usage of Assert.AreEqual( ) and Assert.IsNull( ).

Methods identified by the attributes TestFixtureSetUp and TestFixtureTearDown act similarly to SetUp and TearDown, but are called only once for a given TestFixture rather than for each test method. This feature is useful when it is undesirable to initialize an object multiple times, such as when creating it is computationally intensive. However, TestFixtureSetUp and TestFixtureTearDown should be used with caution because they introduce the potential for test coupling. If multiple test methods share an object that may change state during the test, the tests are not isolated.

Using TestFixtureSetUp is safe when the shared objects being initialized cannot be affected by the test methods. Example 8-3 shows how TestFixtureSetUp and TestFixtureTearDown could be used in LibraryTest.

Example 8-3. The test class LibraryTest, using TestFixtureSetUp

LibraryTest.cs
```
[TestFixtureSetUp]
public void TestFixtureSetUp()
{
    book1 = new Book( "Cosmos", "Carl Sagan" );
    book2 = new Book( "Contact", "Carl Sagan" );
}

[TestFixtureTearDown]
public void TestFixtureTearDown()
{
}

[SetUp]
public void SetUp()
{
    library = new Library();
    library.addBook(book1);
    library.addBook(book2);
}

[TearDown]
public void TearDown()
{
}
```

Since the Book objects won't be modified by the test methods, they can safely be created in TestFixtureSetUp() without risking test coupling. The test methods can change the state of the Library object, so it must be initialized in SetUp() to guarantee that it is in the same state for each test.

When LibraryTest is run, the sequence of calls is:
```
TestFixtureSetUp()
SetUp()
TestGetBookByTitleAndAuthor()
TearDown()
SetUp()
TestRemoveBook()
TearDown()
TestFixtureTearDown()
```

The TestFixtureSetUp() and TestFixtureTearDown() methods are called once for the test fixture, whereas SetUp() and TearDown() are called for each test method.

NUnit supports writing tests for expected error behavior using the ExpectedException attribute. Example 8-4 shows a LibraryTest test method to check that attempting to remove a nonexistent Book causes an Exception to be thrown.

Example 8-4. The test method TestRemoveNonexistentBook

LibraryTest.cs
```
    [Test]
    [ExpectedException(typeof(Exception))]
    public void TestRemoveNonexistentBook( )
    {
        library.removeBook( "Nonexistent" );
    }
```

The attribute ExpectedException(typeof(Exception)) indicates that the test method is expected to throw an Exception. If an Exception is not thrown, the test fails. The attribute Test still is necessary to indicate that this is a test method.

Another NUnit attribute is Ignore, which specifies that a test method should not be run. This can be useful for temporarily disabling a failing test. Example 8-5 demonstrates its usage.

Example 8-5. The test method TestBadTest

LibraryTest.cs
```
    [Test, Ignore("Bad test")]
    public void TestBadTest( )
    {
        Assert.Fail( "Always fails" );
    }
```

Since the test method TestBadTest( ) has the Ignore attribute, NUnit will not run it. Attributes can be combined, as shown by the compound Test and Ignore attributes.

NUnit tests are run using the NUnit GUI or a console test runner. When using the GUI, the File → Open menu command is used to open the *.DLL* or *.EXE* file containing the unit tests. The tests found are displayed in the GUI as a hierarchy of test fixtures and test methods. The Run button executes the tests and displays their results, as shown in Figure 8-1.

Successful tests are flagged green and failures are red. Tests marked with the Ignore attribute are not run and are flagged with a yellow mark. The status bar on the right indicates the overall result: green if everything succeeds, red if there is a failure, and yellow if any tests are skipped.

Running tests using the console test runner is similar, as shown in Example 8-6.

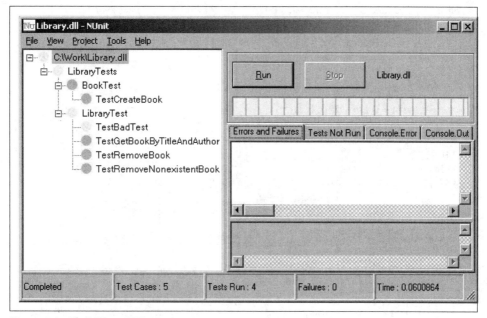

Figure 8-1. The NUnit GUI

Example 8-6. Running tests using the NUnit console

```
>nunit-console.exe C:\Work\Library.dll

.....N
Tests run: 4, Failures: 0, Not run: 1, Time: 0.050072 seconds

Tests not run:
LibraryTests.LibraryTest.TestBadTest : Bad test
```

Test failures and tests that are not run are reported, along with the total number of tests.

The C# class Book referred to in this chapter is shown in Example 8-7.

Example 8-7. The class Book

Book.cs
```
using System;

namespace Library
{
    public class Book
    {
        public string title;
        public string author;

        public Book(string title, string author)
        {
```

Example 8-7. The class Book (continued)

```
        this.title = title;
        this.author = author;
    }
  }
}
```

The class Library is shown in Example 8-8.

Example 8-8. The class Library

```
Library.cs
using System;
using System.Collections;

namespace Library
{
   public class Library
   {
      private Hashtable books;

      public Library( )
      {
         books = new Hashtable( );
      }

      public void addBook(Book book)
      {
         books.Add( book.title, book );
      }

      public Book getBook(string title, string author)
      {
         return (Book)books[ title ];
      }

      public void removeBook(string title)
      {
         if ( books[ title ] == null )
            throw new Exception( "book not found" );
         books.Remove( title );
      }
   }
}
```

Test Assert Methods

NUnit provides a variety of test assert methods. Each one has a variant taking a message parameter, which appears as a descriptive message when the test fails.

The test assert methods referenced here are static methods of the class Assert. Additional test assert methods exist in the class Assertion, but they are obsolete and not recommended for use.

```
IsTrue(bool condition)
IsTrue(bool condition, string message)
```
Test passes if condition is true. This is the most generic type of assert.

```
IsFalse(bool condition)
IsFalse(bool condition, string message)
```
Test passes if condition is false.

```
AreEqual(decimal expected, decimal actual)
AreEqual(decimal expected, decimal actual, string message)
AreEqual(int expected, int actual)
AreEqual(int expected, int actual, string message)
```
Test passes if expected and actual are numerically equal.

```
AreEqual(double expected, double actual, double delta)
AreEqual(double expected, double actual, double delta, string message)
AreEqual(float expected, float actual, float delta)
AreEqual(float expected, float actual, float delta, string message)
```
Test passes if expected and actual are numerically equal within a tolerance of delta. If delta is 0, exact equality is necessary for test to pass.

```
AreEqual(Object expected, Object actual)
AreEqual(Object expected, Object actual, string message)
```
Test passes if expected and actual are equal. If both are numeric types, they are tested for numerical equality. Otherwise, the method Object.equals( ) is used to test equality.

```
AreSame(Object expected, Object actual)
AreSame(Object expected, Object actual, string message)
```
Test passes if expected and actual refer to the same Object.

```
IsNotNull(Object anObject)
IsNotNull(Object anObject, string message)
```
Test passes if anObject is not null.

```
IsNull(Object anObject)
IsNull(Object anObject, string message)
```
Test passes if anObject is null.

```
Fail( )
Fail(string message)
```
Test assert that always fails.

CHAPTER 9

PyUnit

Overview

PyUnit brings xUnit to Python. Python is an interpreted, interactive, object-oriented programming language, widely used for many different kinds of software development. Steve Purcell ported JUnit to Python to create PyUnit. It follows the generic xUnit model closely. The standard Python libraries have included PyUnit since Python 2.1.

Python is open source software that is copyrighted but freely usable and distributable. PyUnit has the same terms as Python itself, with a stipulation that Steve Purcell be credited as the author in the source code and any accompanying documentation.

For more information about Python, see *http://www.python.org*. PyUnit's home is *http://pyunit.sourceforge.net*. The information in this chapter is based on Python 2.3.3, which includes Version 1.4.6 of PyUnit.

Architecture

PyUnit's architecture is simple and effective. Tests are implemented by inheritance from a base class, TestCase, which supports test fixture behavior. Tests may be aggregated using a TestSuite. A number of test assert methods are provided. The PyUnit module, unittest.py, not only contains the foundation code for building unit tests, but also acts as a test runner to execute tests from the command line. A GUI test runner is also provided.

Usage

Test classes are created by subclassing TestCase. The simplest approach is to override the method runTest( ), as shown in Example 9-1.

Example 9-1. Simple unit test for the class Book

booktests.py
```
"""Unit test for book.py"""

import book
import unittest

class BookTests(unittest.TestCase):

    def runTest(self):
        """Test book creation"""
        book1 = book.Book( "Cosmos", "Carl Sagan" )
        self.assertEqual( "Cosmos", book1.title )
```

This example creates the test class BookTests. The test method runTest( ) creates a Book and uses the assertEqual( ) test assert method to verify its attributes. Test methods customarily contain a label similar to the example's Test book creation. This test description is printed if the test fails.

The class Book tested by BookTests is given in Example 9-2.

Example 9-2. Simple unit test for the class Book

book.py

```
class Book:
    title = ""
    author = ""

    def __init__(self, title, author):
        self.title = title
        self.author = author
```

Unit tests may be run from the command line using unittests.py as a test runner. The argument specifies the Python module name, class name, and method name of the test to run. Example 9-3 demonstrates running BookTests this way and shows the result.

Example 9-3. Results of running BookTests

```
$ python unittest.py booktests.BookTests.runTest
.
------------------------------------------------
Ran 1 test in 0.000s

OK
```

For this command to work as shown, the module unittests.py must be present in the Python search path specified by the environment variable $PYTHONPATH.

Making BookTests fail by changing the test assert statement to self.assertEqual ("Bad", book1.title) demonstrates PyUnit's test failure reporting, as shown in Example 9-4.

Example 9-4. BookTests failure

```
$ python unittest.py booktests.BookTests.runTest
F
======================================================================
FAIL: Test book creation
----------------------------------------------------------------------
Traceback (most recent call last):
  File "/cygdrive/c/work/UnitTestFrameworks/Python/example1/booktests.py", line 11, in
runTest
    self.assertEqual( "Bad", book1.title )
  File "/cygdrive/c/work/UnitTestFrameworks/Python/example1/unittest.py", line 302, in
failUnlessEqual
    raise self.failureException, \
AssertionError: 'Bad' != 'Cosmos'


----------------------------------------------------------------------
Ran 1 test in 0.000s

FAILED (failures=1)
```

The failure report includes the test description Test book creation, as well as the specific assert condition that failed.

Rather than overriding runTest( ), it is far more common to create uniquely named test methods. This allows building test classes with multiple test methods. Example 9-5 shows BookTests redesigned this way.

Example 9-5. Redesigned BookTest

booktests.py
```
"""Unit test for book.py"""

import book
import unittest

class BookTests(unittest.TestCase):

    def testCreateBook(self):
        """Test book creation"""
        book1 = book.Book( "Cosmos", "Carl Sagan" )
        self.assertEqual( "Cosmos", book1.title )

if __name__ == '__main__':
    unittest.main( )
```

The additional two lines of code at the end allow the test to be run directly without using unittest.py, as shown in Example 9-6. All methods that have names starting with test are found and run.

Example 9-6. Running BookTest directly

```
$ python booktests.py
.
---------------------
Ran 1 test in 0.000s

OK
```

With this approach, multiple test methods can be added to a test class. If they share objects, test fixture behavior should be implemented using the setUp( ) and tearDown( ) methods. Example 9-7 shows the test fixture LibraryTests.

Example 9-7. . The test class LibraryTests

librarytests.py
```
"""Unit test for library.py"""

import book
import library
import unittest

class LibraryTests(unittest.TestCase):

    def setUp(self):
        self.library = library.Library( )
        book1 = book.Book( "Cosmos", "Carl Sagan" )
        self.library.addBook( book1 )
        book2 = book.Book( "Contact", "Carl Sagan" )
        self.library.addBook( book2 )

    def tearDown(self):
        self.library.dispose( )

    def testGetNumBooks(self):
        """Test getting number of books"""
        self.assert_( self.library.getNumBooks( )==2 )

    def testGetBook(self):
        """Test getting a book from library"""
        book2 = self.library.getBook( "Cosmos" )
        self.assertNotEqual( None, book2, "Book not found" )
```

The setUp( ) method creates a Library and adds two Books to it, and tearDown( ) disposes of the Library. The test method testGetNumBooks( ) uses the test assert method assert_( ) to check the library's size. This is the most generic type of test assert, as it simply checks whether its argument evaluates to true.

Example 9-8 shows the Library class that is tested by LibraryTest.

Example 9-8. The Library class

library.py
```
class NonexistentBookError(Exception):
```

Example 9-8. The Library class (continued)

```
    """Exception thrown for missing book"""
    pass

class Library:
    """A library"""

    def __init__(self):
        self.__books = dict()

    def dispose(self):
        self.__books.clear()

    def addBook(self, book):
        """Add a book"""
        self.__books[book.title] = book

    def getBook(self, title):
        """Find a book by title"""
        return self.__books.get(title)

    def removeBook(self, title):
        """Remove a book"""
        if self.__books.has_key(title):
            self.__books.pop(title)
        else:
            raise NonexistentBookError

    def getNumBooks(self):
        """Get number of books"""
        return len(self.__books)
```

Library uses the Python dictionary object dict() to contain a collection of Books. The module library.py also defines the exception class NonexistentBookError. This type of exception is thrown by the method removeBook() if it cannot find the Book to remove.

The failUnlessRaises() test assert method can be used to check for expected exception behavior, as shown in Example 9-9.

Example 9-9. Testing for an expected exception

librarytests.py
```
    def testRemoveNonexistentBook(self):
        """Test expected exception from removing a nonexistent book"""
        self.failUnlessRaises(library.NonexistentBookError,
            self.library.removeBook, "Nonexistent" )
```

The arguments passed to failUnlessRaises() are an exception type, a callable object, and a variable argument list. In this example, the exception type is NonexistentBookError and the callable object is the function removeBook(). The object is called with the specified argument list. If an exception of the given exception type is thrown, the test passes. If no exception is thrown, or some other type of error occurs, the test fails.

Multiple tests may be aggregated using TestSuite. Example 9-10 adds a function named suite( ) to create a TestSuite containing LibraryTest's test methods and changes the call to run the suite to unittest.main( ).

Example 9-10. Creating and running a TestSuite

librarytests.py
```
def suite():
    suite = unittest.TestSuite()
    suite.addTest(LibraryTests("testGetNumBooks"))
    suite.addTest(LibraryTests("testGetBook"))
    suite.addTest(LibraryTests("testRemoveNonexistentBook"))
    return suite

if __name__ == '__main__':
    unittest.main(defaultTest='suite')
```

Tests are added to a TestSuite using its addTest( ) method. It also has an addTests( ) method that allows multiple tests to be added at once.

PyUnit provides a convenience method, makeSuite( ), which creates a TestSuite. It finds all methods named with a given prefix, such as test, and returns a suite containing them. Example 9-11 demonstrates makeSuite( ).

Example 9-11. . Using makeSuite() to create a TestSuite

librarytests.py
```
def suite():
    suite = unittest.makeSuite(LibraryTests, "test")
    return suite
```

It's often useful to create a module that builds TestSuite containing all the tests in each test class. Example 9-12 shows such a module, named alltests.py.

Example 9-12. Module to run all tests

alltests.py
```
import unittest

def suite():
    modules_to_test = ('booktests', 'librarytests')
    alltests = unittest.TestSuite()
    for module in map(__import__, modules_to_test):
        alltests.addTest(unittest.findTestCases(module))
    return alltests

if __name__ == '__main__':
    unittest.main(defaultTest='suite')
```

This example creates and runs a `TestSuite` named `alltests` that contains all the tests from `booktests.py` and `librarytests.py`.

Python includes a command-line interpreter for interactively running code. PyUnit tests can be run this way. Example 9-13 demonstrates using the interpreter to create and run a unit test.

Example 9-13. Running a test interactively

```
$ python
>>> import unittest
>>> import librarytests
>>> runner = unittest.TextTestRunner( )
>>> test = librarytests.LibraryTests("testGetBook")
>>> runner.run(test)
.
-----------------------------------------------------------------------
Ran 1 test in 0.000s

OK
<unittest._TextTestResult run=1 errors=0 failures=0>
```

In this example, the modules `unittest` and `librarytests` are imported and a `TextTestRunner` is created. Next, a test containing the test method `testGetBook( )` is created and run using the test runner.

A `TestSuite` can be created and run similarly, as shown in Example 9-14.

Example 9-14. Creating a TestSuite interactively

```
>>> suite = unittest.makeSuite(librarytests.LibraryTests,'test')
>>> runner.run(suite)
.....
-----------------------------------------------------------------------
Ran 5 tests in 0.001s

OK
<unittest._TextTestResult run=5 errors=0 failures=0>
```

Example 9-15 illustrates creating a test from `BookTests` and adding it to the `TestSuite`.

Example 9-15. Adding a test to the test suite

```
>>> import booktests
>>> test2 = booktests.BookTests("testCreateBook")
>>> suite.addTest(test2)
>>> runner.run(suite)
......
-----------------------------------------------------
Ran 6 tests in 0.001s

OK
<unittest._TextTestResult run=6 errors=0 failures=0>
```

The PyUnit GUI is implemented in the module unittestgui.py. It is not included with the standard Python libraries but is available in downloads from the PyUnit web site. It acts as a test runner, running test modules, classes, and methods, and displays a friendly green or red test results indicator, as well as failure details. It is shown in Figure 9-1.

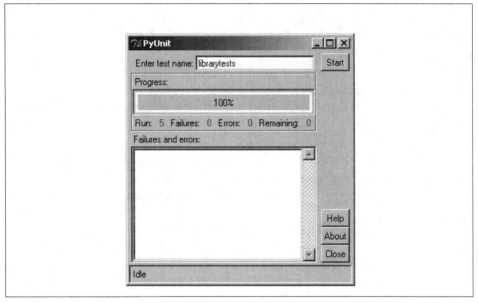

Figure 9-1. The PyUnit GUI

The name of the test to run is entered at the top. The name can specify a module (e.g., librarytests), a test class (librarytests.LibraryTests), or a test method (librarytests.LibraryTests.testGetBook). Except when a specific test method name is specified, all the methods in the module or class being tested that have names starting with test are run.

Test Assert Methods

PyUnit provides 18 test assert methods. Many of them are aliases for the same methods. Most take an optional descriptive message argument, which is reported in case of test failure.

The test assert methods are defined within the class TestCase and are described in the following list. Their first argument, self, is a reference to the TestCase instance. When invoking these methods within a test method, this argument is implicit and does not need to be passed.

```
assert_(self, expr, msg=None)
failUnless(self, expr, msg=None)
```
    Test passes if expr is true. This is the most generic assert method.

```
assertEqual(self, first, second, msg=None)
assertEquals(self, first, second, msg=None)
failUnlessEqual(self, first, second, msg=None)
```
   Test passes if first and second are equal when compared using ==.

```
assertNotEqual(self, first, second, msg=None)
assertNotEquals(self, first, second, msg=None)
failIfEqual(self, first, second, msg=None)
```
   Test fails if first and second are equal when compared using ==.

```
assertAlmostEqual(self, first, second, places=7, msg=None)
assertAlmostEquals(self, first, second, places=7, msg=None)
failUnlessAlmostEqual(self, first, second, places=7, msg=None)
```
   Test passes if first and second are equal after being rounded to places decimal
   places.

```
assertNotAlmostEqual(self, first, second, places=7, msg=None)
assertNotAlmostEquals(self, first, second, places=7, msg=None)
failIfAlmostEqual(self, first, second, places=7, msg=None)
```
   Test fails if first and second are equal after being rounded to places decimal
   places.

```
assertRaises(self, excClass, callableObj, *args, **kwargs)
failUnlessRaises(self, excClass, callableObj, *args, **kwargs)
```
   Call callableObj with arguments args and keyword arguments kwargs. This
   assert passes if an exception of type excClass is thrown.

```
fail(self, msg=None)
```
   Test assert that always fails.

```
failIf(self, expr, msg=None)
```
   Test fails if expr is true.

CHAPTER 10

XMLUnit

Overview

XMLUnit provides useful support for unit testing of XML content. It is an extension to JUnit and NUnit, rather than a standalone framework.

Development and testing of software that generates XML content are common activities. Writing such tests is difficult with generic unit test frameworks. XML tests often compare expected XML content to actual XML content generated by the software that is being tested. Such tests can be written by doing a string comparison between the expected and actual XML content strings. However, what if the actual XML content contains a return character for readability, or puts XML attributes in opposite order than they appear in the expected XML string? Taken as XML documents, the two XML strings have the same contents, but an exact string comparison will fail.

To further illustrate the problem, the following pieces of XML represent an element named book containing the child elements title and author. Since the child elements are not in the same order, these XML elements have equivalent content, but different syntax:

```
<book> <title>Dune</title> <author>Frank Herbert</author> </book>
<book> <author>Frank Herbert</author> <title>Dune</title> </book>
```

The following representations of an empty XML element named library also have equal content but different syntax:

```
<library> </library>
<library/>
```

It is clearly useful to be able to test that two pieces of XML have the same content despite differences in format.

Other common test cases include verifying XML document validity and extracting the value of a particular node in a document, both of which involve writing a lot of code when building upon the generic xUnit test assert methods.

Thus, it is very useful to add knowledge of XML content, parsing, and validity to a unit test framework. XMLUnit addresses this need with a set of functional and powerful tests for XML content.

XMLUnit is open source software authored by Tim Bacon and Jeff Martin. It is released under a BSD license that freely allows redistribution and use of the source and binary code in both original and modified versions, as long as the original copyright notice is included. See the license file included with XMLUnit for full details.

For more information about XMLUnit, see *http://xmlunit.sourceforge.net*. The information in this chapter is based on XMLUnit for Java 1.0. The NUnit version, XMLUnit .Net 0.3, is very similar but is at an earlier stage of development.

Architecture

XMLUnit is implemented as a number of classes built upon the foundation provided by JUnit (or NUnit.) Tests are implemented by inheritance from a base class, XMLTestCase, which is derived from TestCase. The tests may use XML-specific test assert methods from the class XMLAssert.

Java can process XML using any classes compliant with the Java API for XML Processing (JAXP) specification. System properties can be set to name the parser classes to use, as shown here:

```
System.setProperty("javax.xml.parsers.DocumentBuilderFactory",
"org.apache.xerces.jaxp.DocumentBuilderFactoryImpl");
System.setProperty("javax.xml.parsers.SAXParserFactory",
"org.apache.xerces.jaxp.SAXParserFactoryImpl");
```

These calls tell Java to use the Xerces XML parser and document builder.

For XPath and XSL operations, Java can use any XML transformation class that is compliant with the Transformation API for XML (TrAX). Another system property names the transformation class to use:

```
System.setProperty("javax.xml.transform.TransformerFactory",
"org.apache.xalan.processor.TransformerFactoryImpl");
```

This call causes the Xalan transformation engine to be used for XML transformations.

If these properties are not set, the default JAXP parser settings are used. The Apache Crimson XML parser currently ships with Java. Crimson implements neither the World Wide Web Consortium (W3C) DocumentTraversal interface nor the JAXP javax.xml.transform hierarchy. So, it's necessary to use alternative XML tools such as Xerces and Xalan to write XMLUnit tests that do XML transformations or XML tree-walking using DocumentTraversal.

Usage

A basic XMLUnit test verifies that two XML strings are equivalent using the assert method assertXMLEqual( ). The test class is derived from XMLTestCase, which also gives it access to the functionality of the base JUnit class TestCase. Example 10-1 illustrates such a test.

Example 10-1. Testing for equivalent XML content

XMLElementTest.java
```
import org.custommonkey.xmlunit.*;

public class XMLElementTest extends XMLTestCase {

    public void testEmptyElement() throws Exception {
        XMLElement element = new XMLElement("test");
        String expected = "<test></test>";
        assertXMLEqual(expected, element.toString());
    }
}
```

This example creates the test class XMLElementTest to test the class XMLElement. The test method testEmptyElement( ) creates an XMLElement named test and uses the assertXMLEqual( ) test assert method to verify its contents. Since the assert method may throw an Exception, the test method declaration also states that an Exception may be thrown. If the Exception is thrown, the unit test framework will catch the Exception and indicate that the test resulted in an error.

The tested class XMLElement is given in Example 10-2. It represents an XML element.

Example 10-2. The class XMLElement

XMLElement.java

```
public class XMLElement {

    private String name;

    XMLElement(String n) {
        name = n;
    }

    public String toString() {
        return "<"+name+"/>";
    }
}
```

This initial version of XMLElement only knows how to represent an empty element. Its toString() method returns the XML string <test/>. Since assertXMLEquals( ) tests for syntactical equivalence, not literal string equivalence, comparing this string to the expected value <test></test> succeeds. Both strings are valid XML representations of an empty element named test.

A test can also verify that two XML strings are literally identical. All XMLUnit comparison tests use the class `Diff` to compare XML strings. The `assertXMLEquals()` method creates an instance of `Diff` and calls its method `similar()` to check if the two strings are equivalent. To test for identical XML strings, a `Diff` is created and passed to `assertXMLIdentical()`, as shown in Example 10-3.

Example 10-3. Testing for identical XML content

XMLElementTest.java
```
    public void testEmptyElementIdentical() throws Exception {
        XMLElement element = new XMLElement("test");
        String expected = "<test/>";
        Diff diff = new Diff(expected, element.toString());
        assertXMLIdentical(diff, true);
    }
```

The second argument to `assertXMLIdentical()`, the Boolean `TRUE`, indicates that the test should pass if the XML strings are identical. Passing `FALSE` indicates that the test should pass if the strings are not identical.

An XML element can have both text content and child elements. Example 10-4 demonstrates unit tests for adding contents and children to `XMLElement`.

Example 10-4. Test adding content and children to XMLElement

XMLElementTest.java
```
    public void testContent() throws Exception {
        XMLElement element = new XMLElement("test", "content");
        String expected = "<test>content</test>";
        assertXMLEqual(expected, element.toString());
    }

    public void testAddChildren() throws Exception {
        XMLElement element = new XMLElement("test");
        XMLElement child = new XMLElement("child", "content");
        XMLElement child2 = new XMLElement("child2", "content2");
        element.addChild( child );
        element.addChild( child2 );
        String expected =
            "<test><child>content</child><child2>content2</child2></test>";
        assertXMLEqual(expected, element.toString());
    }
```

Again, `assertXMLEqual()` is used to verify the XML produced by `XMLElement`. The new behaviors being tested are the generation of XML for an element with text content and for an element with two children, each with their own text content.

Example 10-5 implements `XMLElement` to support adding text content and children to an element.

Example 10-5. Version of XMLElement supporting text content and child elements

XMLElement.java
```java
import java.util.*;

public class XMLElement {

    private String name;
    private String content;
    private Vector children;
    XMLElement(String n) {
        name = n;
        content = "";
        children = new Vector();
    }

    XMLElement(String n, String c) {
        name = n;
        content = c;
        children = new Vector();
    }

    public void addChild(XMLElement child) {
        children.addElement( child );
    }

    public String toString() {
        if ( content.length() == 0 && children.size() == 0 )
            return "<"+name+"/>";
        else {
            String result = "<"+name+">"+content;
            for (Enumeration e = children.elements();
                    e.hasMoreElements(); ) {
                XMLElement element = (XMLElement)e.nextElement();
                result += element.toString();
            }
            result += "</"+name+">";
            return result;
        }
    }
}
```

A new XMLElement constructor allows content to be specified when an element is created. The method addChild( ) allows child elements to be added.

Testing individual XML elements is relatively easy. When it is necessary to unit test entire XML documents, XMLUnit really shows its usefulness. It supports building tests that compare and validate documents, as well as extracting and validating a document's nodes. With this test support, the task of building a custom XML document format becomes well-suited to test driven development methods. It makes sense to first test and build the functionality to write an empty document and then, as elements and attributes are added to the document format, to write additional tests for them.

The design of an XML document format is codified in a *Document Type Definition* (DTD). A DTD contains the specification for a particular document type in terms of both the elements it may contain and the contents of those elements. Elements may contain attributes, text contents, and child elements. An XML document may contain its own DTD as part of its header information, or it may contain a reference to another file where the DTD is found. It is a matter of personal choice whether you write unit tests that specifically test the contents of the DTD. Regardless of whether the DTD itself is tested, its validity is indirectly verified by unit tests that check the validity of XML documents that use it.

The most basic XMLUnit test to verify a document is assertXMLValid( ). It takes an XML document represented as a string, parses it, and fails if there are any errors. Example 10-6 demonstrates validation of an XML document using this assertion.

Example 10-6. Test using assertXMLValid to validate an XML document

LibraryXMLDocTest.java
```
import org.custommonkey.xmlunit.*;

public class LibraryXMLDocTest extends XMLTestCase {

    public void testValid( ) throws Exception {
        Library library = new Library( );
        LibraryXMLDoc doc = new LibraryXMLDoc( library );
        assertXMLValid( doc.toString( ) );
    }
}
```

This test creates an instance of the new class LibraryXMLDoc and tests the validity of the XML document created by its toString( ) method. To pass the assertXMLValid( ) test, an XML document must contain a DOCTYPE definition, a DTD defining an element type, and a root element. Example 10-7 shows the simplest implementation of LibraryXMLDoc that will pass this test.

Example 10-7. Simple version of LibraryXMLDoc to produce a valid XML document

LibraryXMLDoc.java
```
public class LibraryXMLDoc {

    public String toString( ) {
        return "<!DOCTYPE library ["
            + "<!ELEMENT library (#PCDATA) >]>"
            + "<library/>";
    }
}
```

The XML document produced contains a DTD specifying the DOCTYPE library and an element type also named library. It contains one empty library element as well.

Since a Library contains Books, the LibraryXMLDoc DTD logically specifies a root library element containing book elements. A book element has child title and author elements.

Example 10-8 shows the DTD for the library XML document implemented by LibraryXMLDoc.

Example 10-8. The library document DTD

```
<!DOCTYPE library [
    <!ELEMENT library (book*) >
    <!ELEMENT book (title,author) >
    <!ELEMENT title (#PCDATA) >
    <!ELEMENT author (#PCDATA) >
]>
```

This DTD specifies a document format in which a library element contains zero or more book elements, a book contains title and author elements, and the title and author elements contain character data.

Example 10-9 shows a unit test for an XML document that is compliant with this DTD. The document should contain a library element, which contains a book element. This in turn contains title and author elements. At this point, it also makes sense to refactor LibraryXMLDocTest into a fixture to reduce code duplication between tests.

Example 10-9. Testing the library, book, title, and author elements

```
LibraryXMLDocTest.java
import java.io.*;
import org.w3c.dom.*;
import javax.xml.parsers.*;
import org.xml.sax.InputSource;
import org.custommonkey.xmlunit.*;

public class LibraryXMLDocTest extends XMLTestCase {

    private Library library;
    private DocumentBuilder builder;

    public void setUp() throws Exception {
        library = new Library();
        DocumentBuilderFactory builderFactory =
            DocumentBuilderFactory.newInstance();
        builder = builderFactory.newDocumentBuilder();
    }

    public void testReadDocOneBook() throws Exception {
        library.addBook(new Book("On the Road", "Jack Kerouac"));
        LibraryXMLDoc doc = new LibraryXMLDoc( library );
        InputSource in =
            new InputSource(new StringReader( doc.toString() ));
```

```
        Document response = builder.parse( in );
        NodeList books = response.getElementsByTagName("book");
        assertEquals(1, books.getLength( ));
        Node bookNode = books.item(0);
        Node titleNode = bookNode.getFirstChild( );
        Text titleText = (Text)titleNode.getFirstChild( );
        Node authorNode = bookNode.getLastChild( );
        Text authorText = (Text)authorNode.getFirstChild( );
        assertEquals("On the Road", titleText.getData( ));
        assertEquals("Jack Kerouac", authorText.getData( ));
    }
}
```

The test method testReadDocOneBook( ) relies on several external objects to parse the XML document. These include a javax.xml.parsers.DocumentBuilder parser and Document, NodeList, Node, and Text objects to contain the parsed XML entities. Using these constructs, the test obtains the book, title, and author elements, and verifies the title and author text contents.

For the implementation of LibraryXMLDoc to pass these tests, see the end of this section.

The previous example parses a document and extracts individual node values. To avoid tedious repetitions of this kind of code, XMLUnit offers support for automatically walking the XML node tree with the NodeTest class and the NodeTester interface. Using this feature requires using an XML implementation that supports the DocumentTraversal interface, such as the Xerces parser.

Example 10-10 shows a unit test that uses NodeTest and NodeTester to walk the tree and check the element names and text content values.

Example 10-10. Walking the tree to test node values

LibraryXMLDocTest.java

```
    public void testWalkTree( ) throws Exception {
        XMLUnit.setControlParser(
            "org.apache.xerces.jaxp.DocumentBuilderFactoryImpl");
        library.addBook(new Book("title1", "author1"));
        library.addBook(new Book("title2", "author2"));
        LibraryXMLDoc doc3 = new LibraryXMLDoc( library );
        String testDoc = doc3.toString( );
        NodeTest nodeTest = new NodeTest(testDoc);
        assertNodeTestPasses(nodeTest, new LibraryNodeTester( ),
            new short[] {Node.TEXT_NODE, Node.ELEMENT_NODE}, true);
    }

    private class LibraryNodeTester extends AbstractNodeTester {

        private String currName = "";

        public void testText(Text text) throws NodeTestException {
```

Example 10-10. Walking the tree to test node values (continued)

```
        String txt = text.getData();
        System.out.println("text="+txt);
        if ((currName.equals("title")
             && txt.substring(0,5).equals("title"))
          || (currName.equals("author")
             && txt.substring(0,6).equals("author")))
            return;
        throw new NodeTestException("Incorrect text value", text);
    }

    public void testElement(Element element)
        throws NodeTestException {
        String name = element.getLocalName();
        System.out.println("name="+name);
        if (!name.equals("library") && !name.equals("book")
            && !name.equals("title") && !name.equals("author"))
            throw new NodeTestException("Unexpected name", element);
        if (name.equals("title") || name.equals("author"))
            currName = name;
    }

    public void noMoreNodes(NodeTest nodeTest)
        throws NodeTestException {}
}
```

The test method is named testWalkTree(). It first calls setControlParser() to use the Xerces parser. Next, it adds two Books to the Library and creates a LibraryXMLDoc. An instance of NodeTest is created with the XML document string as its argument. The assert method assertNodeTestPasses() is called. This method takes an AbstractNodeTester as an argument, along with an array of Node types telling it which XML nodes to test.

The rest of the example is a custom AbstractNodeTester class named LibraryNodeTester that performs the actual testing of Node values. The method testElement() receives Element objects and the method testText() receives Text objects. In this example, the Elements are tested to verify they are either named library, book, title, or author, and the Text objects are tested to verify they contain the string title or author.

The following output from running the test demonstrates how it works. The NodeTest object traverses the document tree and passes all of the elements and text contents to LibraryNodeTester:

```
$ java junit.textui.TestRunner LibraryXMLDocTest
.name=library
name=book
name=title
text=title2
name=author
text=author2
```

```
name=book
name=title
text=title1
name=author
text=author1
```

A useful addition to the XML specification is the *XML Path Language*, known as XPath. It allows XML documents to be queried and manipulated using a URL-like path notation. XMLUnit offers a number of test assert methods that verify the results of XPath statements. Example 10-11 shows a unit test that creates XPath expressions to find book elements in a library XML document, and compares their results.

Example 10-11. Testing XPath expressions

LibraryXMLDocTest.java
```
   public void testXpath( ) throws Exception {
      library.addBook(new Book("On the Road", "Jack Kerouac"));
      library.addBook(new Book("Dune", "Frank Herbert"));
      LibraryXMLDoc doc = new LibraryXMLDoc( library );
      String xmlTest = doc.toString( );
      assertXpathExists("//book[title='Dune']", xmlTest);
      assertXpathExists("//book[author='Jack Kerouac']", xmlTest);
      assertXpathNotExists("//book[author='Nobody']", xmlTest);
      assertXpathsEqual("//book[title='Dune']",
         "//book[author='Frank Herbert']", xmlTest);
      assertXpathsNotEqual("//book[title='Dune']",
         "//book[title='On the Road']", xmlTest);
   }
```

This test creates XPath expressions to query book elements by title and author, and verifies that the books are found using assertXpathExists( ). It also verifies whether two XPath expressions return the same element using the assert methods assertXpathsEqual() and assertXpathsNotEqual( ).

For more details on XPath, see the official W3C XPath Recommendation at *http://www.w3.org/TR/xpath*.

Test Assert Methods

The descriptions in the following list are based on the Javadocs for the class XMLTestCase, which contains all of the following test assert methods. The test assert methods use the classes Diff, Validator, NodeTest, and NodeTester from the package org.custommonkey.xmlunit. They also use the interface org.w3c.dom.Document and the class java.io.Reader. The fully qualified package names for these classes are omitted here. Most of the assert methods have variants that perform a given test on either a DOM Document or String representation of XML content.

```
assertNodeTestPasses(NodeTest test, NodeTester tester, short[] nodeTypes,
boolean assertion)
```
Executes a NodeTest using a NodeTester for the specified node types. Assert passes if NodeTest passes and assertion is TRUE, or if NodeTest fails and assertion is FALSE.

```
assertNodeTestPasses(String xmlString, NodeTester tester, short nodeType)
```
Executes a NodeTest using a NodeTester for a single node type and asserts that it passes.

```
assertXMLEqual(Diff diff, boolean assertion)
assertXMLEqual(String msg, Diff diff, boolean assertion)
```
Assert that the result of an XML comparison is or is not similar.

```
assertXMLEqual(Document control, Document test)
assertXMLEqual(String err, Document control, Document test)
assertXMLEqual(Reader control, Reader test)
assertXMLEqual(String err, Reader control, Reader test)
assertXMLEqual(String control, String test)
assertXMLEqual(String err,String control, String test)
```
Assert that two XML documents are similar.

```
assertXMLIdentical(Diff diff, boolean assertion)
assertXMLIdentical(String msg, Diff diff, boolean assertion)
```
Assert that the result of an XML comparison is or is not identical.

```
assertXMLNotEqual(Document control, Document test)
assertXMLNotEqual(String err, Document control, Document test)
assertXMLNotEqual(Reader control, Reader test)
assertXMLNotEqual(String err, Reader control, Reader test)
assertXMLNotEqual(String control, String test)
assertXMLNotEqual(String err, String control, String test)
```
Assert that two XML documents are not similar.

```
assertXMLValid(String xmlString)
```
Asserts that xmlString contains valid XML. To pass, it must contain a DOCTYPE declaration, a DTD defining an element type, and at least one root element.

```
assertXMLValid(String xmlString, String systemId)
```
Asserts that xmlString contains valid XML. To pass, it must contain a DOCTYPE declaration and a root element. The test uses systemId to obtain the DTD.

```
assertXMLValid(String xmlString, String systemId, String doctype)
```
Asserts that xmlString contains valid XML. The XML string will be validated with the doctype and systemId specified, regardless of whether it already contains a DOCTYPE declaration.

```
assertXMLValid(Validator validator)
```
Asserts that an instance of org.custommonkey.xmlunit. Validator returns isValid( ) == true.

```
assertXpathEvaluatesTo(String expectedValue, String xpathExpression, Document
    inDocument)
assertXpathEvaluatesTo(String expectedValue, String xpathExpression, String
    inXMLString)
```
Assert the value of an Xpath expression in a DOM Document or XML String.

```
assertXpathExists(String xPathExpression, Document inDocument)
assertXpathExists(String xPathExpression, String inXMLString)
```
Assert that a specific XPath exists in a DOM Document or XML String.

```
assertXpathNotExists(String xPathExpression, Document inDocument)
assertXpathNotExists(String xPathExpression, String inXMLString)
```
Assert that a specific XPath does not exist in a DOM Document or XML String.

```
assertXpathsEqual(String controlXpath, Document controlDocument, String
    testXpath, Document testDocument)
assertXpathsEqual(String controlXpath, String inControlXMLString, String
    testXpath, String inTestXMLString)
```
Assert that the node lists of two XPaths in two DOM Documents or XML strings
are equal.

```
assertXpathsEqual(String controlXpath, String testXpath, Document document)
assertXpathsEqual(String controlXpath, String testXpath, String inXMLString)
```
Assert that the node lists of two XPaths in the same DOM Document or XML
string are equal.

```
assertXpathsNotEqual(String controlXpath, Document controlDocument, String
    testXpath, Document testDocument)
assertXpathsNotEqual(String controlXpath, String inControlXMLString, String
    testXpath, String inTestXMLString)
```
Assert that the node lists of two XPaths in two DOM Documents or XML strings
are not equal.

```
assertXpathsNotEqual(String controlXpath, String testXpath, Document document)
assertXpathsNotEqual(String controlXpath, String testXpath, String
    inXMLString)
```
Assert that the node lists of two XPaths in the same DOM Document or XML
string are not equal.

```
assertXpathValuesEqual(String controlXpath, Document controlDocument, String
    testXpath, Document testDocument)
assertXpathValuesEqual(String controlXpath, String inControlXMLString, String
    testXpath, String inTestXMLString)
```
Assert that the evaluation of two XPaths in two DOM Documents or XML
strings are equal.

```
assertXpathValuesEqual(String controlXpath, String testXpath, Document
    document)
assertXpathValuesEqual(String controlXpath, String testXpath, String
    inXMLString)
```
Assert that the evaluation of two XPaths in the same DOM Document or XML string are equal.

```
assertXpathValuesNotEqual(String controlXpath, Document controlDocument,
    String testXpath, Document testDocument)
assertXpathValuesNotEqual(String controlXpath, String inControlXMLString,
    String testXpath, String inTestXMLString)
```
Assert that the evaluation of two XPaths in two DOM Documents or XML strings are not equal.

```
assertXpathValuesNotEqual(String controlXpath, String testXpath, Document
    document)
assertXpathValuesNotEqual(String controlXpath, String testXpath, String
    inXMLString)
```
Assert that the evaluation of two XPaths in the same DOM Document or XML string are not equal.

CHAPTER 11

Resources

Unit testing is a constantly evolving technology, as are unit testing tools. This section lists some of the most useful written and electronic resources for learning more about unit testing and for keeping up with new developments.

Web Sites

The best source of up to date information about unit testing and tools is the Internet. Hundreds of sites exist, offering test tool downloads, tutorials, forums, articles, and examples. Several of the most prominent sites are described in the following list:

http://www.xprogramming.com
> This site is a great resource for information about Extreme Programming. The Downloads page includes links to virtually every unit test framework and testing-related tool in existence. This is the first place to look for a test framework for a particular language or domain.

http://www.junit.org
> This is the home of the JUnit test framework. It is also a useful resource for other xUnits. It's the place to download JUnit and its extensions, learn how to use them, and read news and articles about new developments.

http://www.testdriven.com
> This site offers a continuous flow of current TDD-related information, including news, articles, book excerpts, and forums.

http://www.extremeprogramming.org
> This site offers a well-organized introduction to XP, unit testing, and related topics.

http://www.agilealliance.com
> This site is a hub for the Agile Development movement, offering an introduction to agile, news, articles, an index of local user groups, and more.

http://www.sourceforge.net
> SourceForge.net is the home of thousands of open source software projects, including many unit testing and test-related tools. Most of these projects are found under the topic SoftwareDevelopment: Build Tools.

http://cppunit.sourceforge.net
> This is the home of CppUnit.

http://pyunit.sourceforge.net
> The home of PyUnit.

http://xmlunit.sourceforge.net
> The home of XMLUnit.

http://www.nunit.org
> This site is the home of NUnit.

http://www.oreilly.com
> O'Reilly's site is a trove of technical information about unit testing and many other software development topics, offering articles, weblogs, conferences, and (of course) books.

Discussion Groups

There's a great deal of ongoing discussion about Agile Development and unit testing, since they are relatively new developments in the world of software. Online discussion groups are great places to learn more, get involved, and get advice about these technologies. A few of the thousands of active groups are listed here. Beyond these, it is not hard to find discussion groups dedicated to particular xUnits.

testdrivendevelopment
> A Yahoo! group is dedicated to discussion of TDD and unit testing. Have a tricky unit testing problem? Want to listen in when unit test gurus discuss the finer points of the technology? Join this group. Find it at *http://groups.yahoo.com/group/testdrivendevelopment/*.

extremeprogramming
> A very active Yahoo! group dedicated to Extreme Programming. This is located at *http://groups.yahoo.com/group/extremeprogramming/*.

refactoring
> Another Yahoo! group, this one oriented towards refactoring and related topics. It is located at *http://groups.yahoo.com/group/refactoring/*.

JUnit
> Another Yahoo! Group, this one is centered on JUnit specifically. It is located at: *http://groups.yahoo.com/group/junit/*.

Books

Numerous books have been published about Agile Development, unit testing, and specific unit test frameworks. A few of them are listed here:

- *Test Driven Development: A Practical Guide*, by David Astels (Prentice Hall)
- *Test Driven Development: By Example*, by Kent Beck (Addison-Wesley)
- *Test-Driven Development in Microsoft .Net*, by James A. Newkirk and Alexei Vorontsov (Microsoft Press)
- *Testing Extreme Programming*, by Lisa Crispin (Addison-Wesley)
- *Pragmatic Unit Testing in C# with NUnit*, by Andy Hunt and Dave Thomas (The Pragmatic Programmers)
- *Pragmatic Unit Testing in Java with JUnit*, by Andy Hunt and Dave Thomas (The Pragmatic Programmers)
- *Unit Testing in Java—How Tests Drive the Code*, by Johannes Link (Morgan Kaufmann)
- *Agile Software Development: Principles, Patterns, and Practices*, by Robert Martin (Prentice Hall)
- *JUnit in Action*, by Vincent Massol and Ted Husted (Manning Publications)

Simple C++ Unit Test Framework

This appendix contains the C++ version of the simple unit test framework example from Chapter 2. The software architecture of the C++ version is identical to that of the Java version. The only variations are those dictated by the differences in language syntax.

The full description of the example is found in Chapter 2. This appendix simply describes how to build and run the C++ version. It assumes that you are using the GNU g++ compiler. Most other C++ compilers should work as well, but the compilation commands may vary from what is shown here.

Example 1: Create a Book

The first example creates the class Book. En route, the unit test framework is built and the first unit test written.

Step 0: Set Up the Unit Test Framework

The framework initially is built on a single class, UnitTest, shown in Figure A-1. The source code for UnitTest includes a header file, *UnitTest.h*, and an implementation file, *UnitTest.cpp*, as shown in Example A-1.

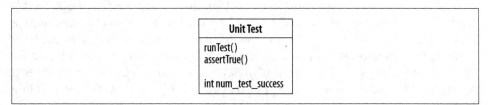

Figure A-1. The class UnitTest

Example A-1. The class UnitTest

UnitTest.h
```
#define UT_ASSERT( condition ) \
    assertTrue(condition,__FILE__,__LINE__,#condition)

class UnitTest {

 public:

   virtual ~UnitTest( ) {}
   virtual void runTest( ) = 0;

 protected:

   void assertTrue(bool condition, const char *file,
                  int line, const char *msg);
   static int num_test_success;

};
```

UnitTest.cpp
```
#include <stdio.h>
#include <stdlib.h>
#include "UnitTest.h"

int UnitTest::num_test_success = 0;

void UnitTest::assertTrue(bool condition,
                          const char *file, int line,
                          const char *msg) {
   if (!(condition)) {
      printf("FAILURE!\n");
      printf("%s:%d:%s\n", file, line, msg);
      exit(1);
   }
   ++num_test_success;

}
```

UnitTest is an abstract class because it contains the pure virtual function runTest( ). Actual unit tests will be inherited from UnitTest and must override the runTest( ) method. The function assertTrue( ) should be used to test Boolean conditions in runTest( ). If the condition is TRUE, the counter num_test_success is incremented. If it is FALSE, the function test_failure( ) is called. This function reports the file location of the failure and exits. The macro UT_ASSERT( ) is used in place of direct calls to assertTrue( ). It uses the preprocessor directives __FILE__ and __LINE__ to fill in the location of the call at compilation, and the #condition argument allows the conditional expression to be printed in the failure report.

Compile UnitTest with the command g++ -c UnitTest.cpp (or your compiler's equivalent command).

Step 1: Create a Unit Test

Start by creating the unit test class BookTest, as shown in Example A-2.

Example A-2. The definition of the class BookTest

BookTest.h
```
#include "UnitTest.h"
#include "Book.h"

class BookTest : public UnitTest {

 public:

    void runTest() {
        Book book("Cosmos");
        UT_ASSERT(!strcmp(book.title, "Cosmos"));
    }

};
```

The unit test BookTest constructs an instance of the class Book, passing the title as an argument, and then tests the value of the book's title attribute. Since the entire implementation of BookTest is present in *BookTest.h*, no *.cpp* file is necessary.

BookTest is instantiated and run by a class called TestRunner, which also contains the main() method for the test framework. Example A-3 shows the implementation of TestRunner.

Example A-3. The class TestRunner

TestRunner.cpp
```
#include "stdio.h"
#include "BookTest.h"

int main() {

    BookTest test;
    test.runTest();
    printf("SUCCESS!\n");
    return 0;

}
```

Compile TestRunner. The compiler will report that it cannot find the file Book.h, and that the class Book is undeclared. No surprise there! So, the next step is to create the most basic implementation of the class Book that will allow the code to compile, as shown in Example A-4.

Example A-4. Initial version of the class Book

Book.h
```
#include "string.h"
```

Example A-4. Initial version of the class Book (continued)

```
class Book {

 public:

   Book(const char* title) {}

   char title[255];

};
```

The class TestRunner should compile now. The test framework and the unit test are in place. To run the test, link the objects together into an executable:

```
g++ -o TestRunner TestRunner.o UnitTest.o
```

Execute TestRunner. The following result is reported:

```
FAILURE!
BookTest.h:9:!strcmp(book.title, "Cosmos")
```

This failure demonstrates that the unit test framework is working. Note how the UT_ASSERT( ) macro captures the file's name and location, as well as the code contents of the test assertion.

Step 2: Create a Book

BookTest fails because Book does not yet contain the functionality being tested. In this step, the minimum necessary code to achieve unit test success is added.

The constructor for Book is changed to set the title attribute, as shown in Example A-5.

Example A-5. The class Book with title attribute set by the constructor

```
Book.h
#include "string.h"

class Book {

 public:

   Book(const char* title) {
      strcpy(this->title, title);
   }

   char title[255];

};
```

Step 3: Test Again

The final step is to rebuild the code, re-run the unit test, and see whether the changes produce the desired results.

Rebuild and execute TestRunner. The results of BookTest are reported:

```
SUCCESS!
```

An instance of Book can now be created and given a title.

Example 2: Create a Library

For the second example, functionality will be added to add a book to a library and retrieve it. These features will be provided by a Library class. To test Library, the unit test should add a Book to a Library and then get that Book from the Library, thus verifying that the Library contains the Book. The unit test framework also will be modified to report the number of tests run.

Step 1: Test Adding a Book to a Library

The initial version of LibraryTest is shown in Example A-6.

Example A-6. Initial version of LibraryTest

LibraryTest.h
```
#include "UnitTest.h"
#include "Library.h"

class LibraryTest : public UnitTest {

 public:

    void runTest() {
       // Create library
       Library library;
       // Add book to library
       Book *book = new Book( "Cosmos" );
       library.addBook( book );
       // Lookup book in library
       Book *book2;
       book2 = library.getBook( "Cosmos" );
       UT_ASSERT( !strcmp(book2->title, "Cosmos") );
    }

};
```

LibraryTest is added to TestRunner, as shown in Example A-7.

Example A-7. TestRunner modified to run LibraryTest

TestRunner.cpp
```
#include "stdio.h"
#include "BookTest.h"
#include "LibraryTest.h"

int main( ) {

    BookTest test;
    test.runTest( );
    LibraryTest test2;
    test2.runTest( );
    printf("SUCCESS!\n");
    printf("%d tests completed successfully\n",
        UnitTest::getNumSuccess( ));
    return 0;

}
```

Now that more than one unit test is being run, it's useful to report the value of the test success counter. To obtain this value, the accessor function getNumSuccess( ) is added to UnitTest. Also, a #define block is added so that the compiler doesn't complain about multiple definitions of UnitTest. Example A-8 shows the changes to UnitTest.

Example A-8. UnitTest with accessor function getNumSuccess

UnitTest.h
```
#ifndef _UNIT_TEST_H_
#define _UNIT_TEST_H_

#define UT_ASSERT( condition ) \
    assertTrue(condition,__FILE__,__LINE__,#condition)

class UnitTest {

 public:

    virtual ~UnitTest( ) {}
    virtual void runTest( ) = 0;
    static int getNumSuccess( ) { return num_test_success; }

 protected:

    void assertTrue(bool condition, const char *file,
                int line, const char *msg);
    static int num_test_success;

};

#endif
```

A minimal "stub" version of the Library class is created so that LibraryTest can be compiled, as shown in Example A-9.

Example A-9. Initial version of Library

Library.h
```
#include "Book.h"

class Library {

 public:
   Library();
   ~Library();

   void addBook( Book *book );
   Book* getBook( const char *title );

};
```

Library.cpp
```
#include "Library.h"

Library::Library() {}

Library::~Library() {}

void Library::addBook( Book* book ) {}

Book* Library::getBook( const char *title ) {
   return new Book("");
}
```

Compiling and running this code produces the expected LibraryTest failure, as well as the BookTest success:

```
FAILURE!
LibraryTest.h:17:!strcmp(book2->title, "Cosmos")
1 tests completed successfully
```

Step 2: Add a Book to a Library

The final step is to add the new functionality to Library and verify that the unit test succeeds.

Example A-10 shows the Library class with the minimum necessary code to pass LibraryTest.

Example A-10. Library with changes to pass LibraryTest

Library.h
```
#include "Book.h"

class Library {
```

Example A-10. Library with changes to pass LibraryTest (continued)

```
public:
  Library( );
  ~Library( );

  void addBook( Book *book );
  Book* getBook( const char *title );

private:
  Book* books;

};
```

Library.cpp
```
#include "Library.h"

Library::Library( ) {
}

Library::~Library( ) {}

void Library::addBook( Book* book ) {
  books = book;
}

Book* Library::getBook( const char *title ) {
  return books;
}
```

Step 3: Check Unit Test Results

Compiling and running this code should demonstrate success for both of the unit tests:

```
SUCCESS!
2 tests completed successfully
```

Note that this example code allocates a new Book but never deletes it, causing a memory leak.

The software architecture of the code in this example is shown in Figure A-2. It is identical to the architecture of the Java version.

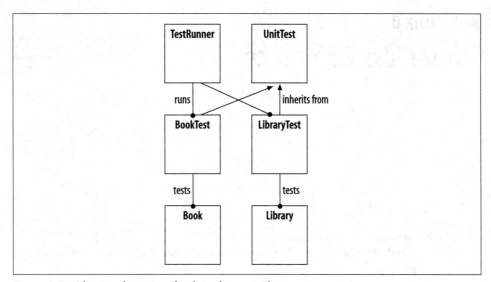

Figure A-2. Object architecture of code in this example

JUnit Class Reference

This appendix provides a reference to the classes in the JUnit package junit. framework. JUnit includes a number of other packages, but its core functionality resides in this package.

In the descriptions in this appendix, the classes Object, String, Error, Class, and Throwable are members of the standard package java.lang. The classes Vector and Enumeration are members of java.util.

Assert

Description

Assert (see Figure B-1) contains only static methods. Its public interface consists solely of unit test assert methods. These methods throw an AssertionFailedError or ComparisonFailure if the test fails. Assert is a parent class of TestCase and other classes that use unit test assert methods.

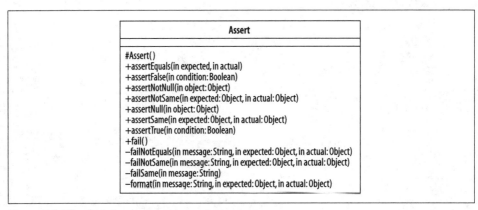

Figure B-1. The class Assert

Declaration

```
public class Assert
extends Object
```

Constructors

```
protected Assert( )
```
Constructor for Assert. It is protected since this is a static class.

Public Methods

```
static void assertEquals(boolean expected, boolean actual)
static void assertEquals(String message, boolean expected, boolean actual)
```
Asserts equality of two boolean values.

```
static void assertEquals(byte expected, byte actual)
static void assertEquals(String message, byte expected, byte actual)
```
Asserts equality of two byte values.

```
static void assertEquals(char expected, char actual)
static void assertEquals(String message, char expected, char actual)
```
Asserts equality of two char values.

```
static void assertEquals(double expected, double actual, double delta)
static void assertEquals(String message, double expected, double actual, double
delta)
```
Asserts equality of two double values within a tolerance of delta. A delta of 0 tests
exact equality.

```
static void assertEquals(float expected, float actual, float delta)
static void assertEquals(String message, float expected, float actual, float delta)
```
Asserts equality of two float values within a tolerance of delta. A delta of 0 tests
exact equality.

```
static void assertEquals(int expected, int actual)
static void assertEquals(String message, int expected, int actual)
```
Asserts equality of two int values.

```
static void assertEquals(long expected, long actual)
static void assertEquals(String message, long expected, long actual)
```
Asserts equality of two long values.

```
static void assertEquals(Object expected, Object actual)
static void assertEquals(String message, Object expected, Object actual)
```
Asserts equality of two Objects using the method Object.equals( ).

```
static void assertEquals(short expected, short actual)
static void assertEquals(String message, short expected, short actual)
```
Asserts equality of two short values.

```
static void assertEquals(String expected, String actual)
static void assertEquals(String message, String expected, String actual)
```
Asserts equality of two Strings using the method String.equals( ).

```
static void assertFalse(boolean condition)
static void assertFalse(String message, boolean condition)
```
Asserts that a boolean condition is false.

```
static void assertNotNull(Object object)
static void assertNotNull(String message, Object object)
```
Asserts that an Object is not null.

```
static void assertNotSame(Object expected, Object actual)
static void assertNotSame(String message, Object expected, Object actual)
```
Asserts that two Objects are not the same Object using the ==" operator.

```
static void assertNull(Object object)
```
```
static void assertNull(String message, Object object)
```
Asserts that an Object is null.

```
static void assertSame(Object expected, Object actual)
static void assertSame(String message, Object expected, Object actual)
```
Asserts that two Objects are the same Object using the == operator.

```
static void assertTrue(boolean condition)
static void assertTrue(String message, boolean condition)
```
Asserts that a condition is true, the most generic type of assertion.

```
static void fail( )
static void fail(String message)
```
Produces a test failure.

Protected/Private Methods

```
private static void failNotEquals(String message, Object expected, Object actual)
private static void failNotSame(String message, Object expected, Object actual)
private static void failSame(String message)
```
Private methods to deal with a test failure by calling fail( ) with a formatted message string.

```
static String format(String message, Object expected, Object actual)
```
Package private method to format a failure message.

Attributes

None.

AssertionFailedError

Description

AssertionFailedError (see Figure B-2) is a class representing an assertion failure. Aside from being a distinct subclass, it is otherwise identical to Error. Thus, it is Throwable and contains a stack trace.

The assert methods in Assert throw an AssertionFailedError (or a subclass of it) when an assertion fails. The AssertionFailedError conveniently captures the stack trace of the code location from which it was thrown, making it easy to find the assertion that failed.

Declaration

```
public class AssertionFailedError
extends java.lang.Error
```

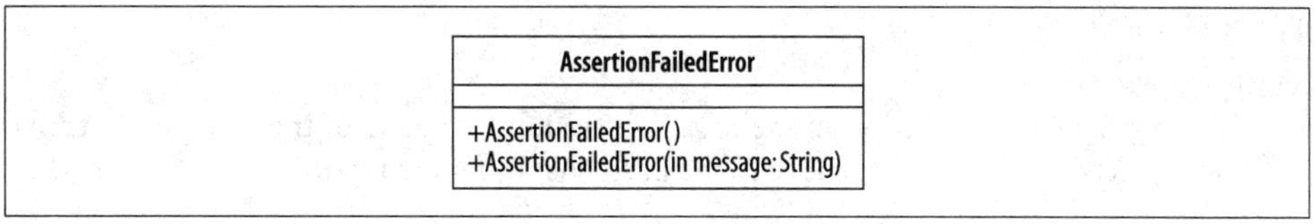

```
┌─────────────────────────────────────────┐
│        ┌─────────────────────────┐        │
│        │    AssertionFailedError  │        │
│        ├─────────────────────────┤        │
│        ├─────────────────────────┤        │
│        │ +AssertionFailedError( ) │        │
│        │ +AssertionFailedError(in message: String) │
│        └─────────────────────────┘        │
└─────────────────────────────────────────┘
```

Figure B-2. The class AssertionFailedError

Constructors

```
public AssertionFailedError( )
public AssertionFailedError(String message)
```
    The constructors for `AssertionFailedError`.

Public Methods

None.

Protected/Private Methods

None.

Attributes

None.

ComparisonFailure

Description

ComparisonFailure (see Figure B-3) is a specialized subclass of AssertionFailedError. It is thrown only by the versions of assertEquals( ) that compare Strings.

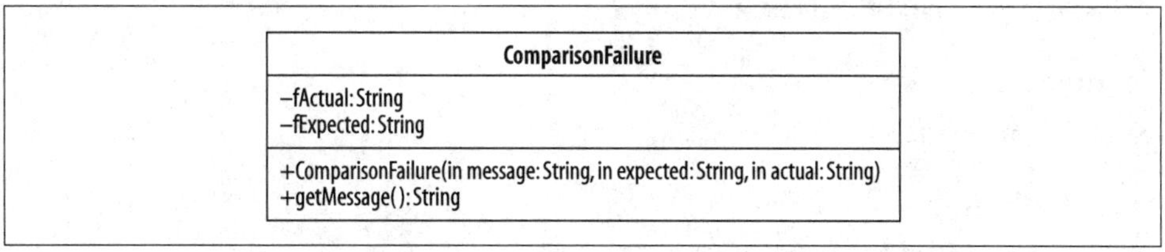

```
┌─────────────────────────────────────────────────────────────┐
│      ┌─────────────────────────────────────────────────┐      │
│      │                ComparisonFailure                 │      │
│      ├─────────────────────────────────────────────────┤      │
│      │ −fActual: String                                 │      │
│      │ −fExpected: String                               │      │
│      ├─────────────────────────────────────────────────┤      │
│      │ +ComparisonFailure(in message: String, in expected: String, in actual: String) │
│      │ +getMessage( ): String                           │      │
│      └─────────────────────────────────────────────────┘      │
└─────────────────────────────────────────────────────────────┘
```

Figure B-3. The class ComparisonFailure

Declaration

```
public class ComparisonFailure
extends AssertionFailedError
```

Constructors

```
ComparisonFailure(String message, String expected, String actual)
```
    The constructor for `ComparisonFailure`.

Public Methods

`String getMessage( )`

> Returns the failure description message. The redundant parts of the compared `String`s are replaced with "..." so that only the parts that differ are reported.

Protected/Private Methods

None.

Attributes

`private String fActual`
`private String fExpected`

> The private attributes containing copies of the strings being compared.

Protectable

Description

Protectable (see Figure B-4) is an interface used by `TestResult` to run test methods in a `Throwable` context.

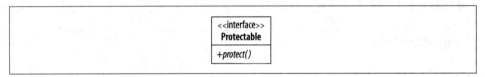

Figure B-4. The interface Protectable

Declaration

`public interface Protectable`

Constructors

None (it's an interface).

Public Methods

`public abstract void protect( ) throws Throwable`

> A class implementing `Protectable` has a public method named `protect( )` that can throw a `Throwable`.

Protected/Private Methods

None.

Attributes

None.

Test

Description

Test (see Figure B-5) is an interface implemented by TestCase and TestSuite. A Test can be run and its results collected in a TestResult. It is an important abstraction, since both individual unit tests and sets of tests are run via the Test interface.

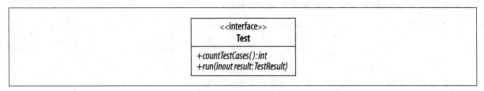

Figure B-5. The interface Test

Declaration

```
public interface Test
```

Constructors

None (it's an interface).

Public Methods

public abstract int countTestCases()
: Returns the number of test cases run by this Test.

public abstract void run(TestResult result)
: Runs the Test and collect its results in a TestResult.

Protected/Private Methods

None.

Attributes

None.

TestCase

Description

TestCase (see Figure B-6) is an abstract class that acts as a parent for unit test classes. A TestCase may contain a single test method or be a test fixture containing multiple tests.

A TestCase may be run directly by calling run( ). More commonly, a TestRunner runs a TestCase by calling run(TestResult), passing in a TestResult object to collect the results.

The method runTest( ) can be overridden by subclasses of TestCase to implement a test class with a single test method.

Alternatively, an instance of TestCase can be created with a name corresponding to the name of a test method. The default implementation of runTest( ) uses reflection to invoke the named test method. This allows a TestCase to have multiple test methods. The following code snippet runs the test method BookTest.testBookTitle( ):

```
TestCase test = new BookTest( "testBookTitle" );
TestResult result = test.run( );
```

Whichever way the test methods are run, TestCase ensures test isolation by running setUp( ) prior to the test method and tearDown( ) afterwards.

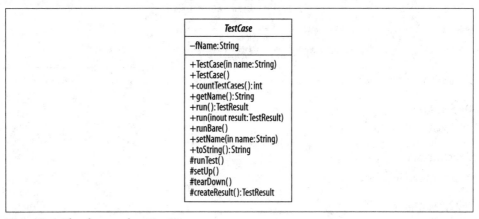

Figure B-6. The abstract class TestCase

Declaration

```
public abstract class TestCase
extends Assert
implements Test
```

Constructors

TestCase(String name)
: A constructor that sets the name. As described above, this name may specify the test method to run.

TestCase( )
: A constructor with no arguments for use in serialization. Should not be used otherwise since it sets the name to null.

Public Methods

int countTestCases( )
: Returns the number of test cases run by this TestCase.

String getName( )
: Gets the name of this TestCase.

TestResult run( )
: Runs this TestCase and returns a new TestResult containing the results. This is a convenience method not normally used by the test framework.

```
void run(TestResult result)
```
Runs this TestCase and collects the results in TestResult.
```
void runBare( ) throws Throwable
```
Runs the test fixture sequence: setUp( ), runTest( ), and tearDown( ).
```
void setName(String name)
```
Sets the name of this TestCase.
```
String toString( )
```
Returns a string representation of the test case.

Protected/Private Methods

```
protected void runTest( ) throws Throwable
```
Runs the unit test and asserts its state using the assert methods from Assert. This method is overridden by subclasses of TestCase, unless reflection is used to run test methods.
```
protected void setUp( ) throws Exception
```
Sets up the test fixture by initializing any objects shared by test methods.
```
protected void tearDown( ) throws Exception
```
Tears down the fixture by cleaning up any shared objects.
```
protected TestResult createResult( )
```
Creates an empty TestResult to collect results. Used by run( ).

Attributes

```
private String fName
```
Provides the name of this TestCase.

TestFailure

Description

TestFailure (see Figure B-7) is a class containing a Test and an associated exception. TestResult produces a TestFailure whenever there is a test failure or error.

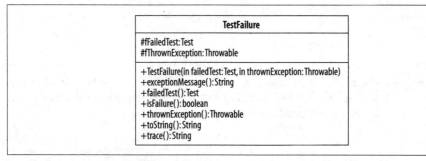

Figure B-7. The class TestFailure

Declaration

```
public class TestFailure
extends Object
```

Constructors

`TestFailure(Test failedTest, Throwable thrownException)`
Constructs a TestFailure for a Test and its exception.

Public Methods

`String exceptionMessage( )`
Gets the exception message.

`Test failedTest( )`
Gets the failed test.

`boolean isFailure( )`
Returns TRUE if the exception is a failure represented by an instance of AssertionFailedError. If FALSE, the test produced an error.

`Throwable thrownException( )`
Gets the exception.

`String toString( )`
Returns a description of the failure consisting of the string Test.toString( ) and the exception message.

`String trace( )`
Returns the stack trace for the exception.

Protected/Private Methods

None.

Attributes

`protected Test fFailedTest`
`protected Throwable fThrownException`
These attributes contain the Test and the exception.

TestListener

Description

TestListener (see Figure B-8) is an interface used for listeners to a TestResult object. A listener may be any class that follows Test progress. Listeners are informed when a Test starts and ends, and when a Test produces a failure or error.

Declaration

```
public interface TestListener
```

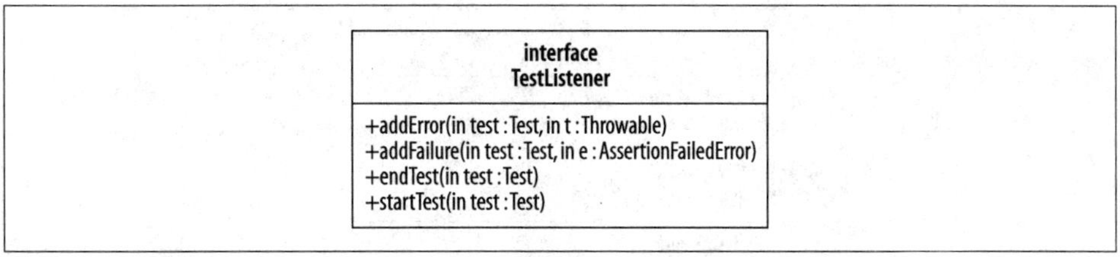

```
┌─────────────────────────────────────────────────────────────┐
│                   ┌──────────────────────────────────────┐   │
│                   │              interface               │   │
│                   │             TestListener             │   │
│                   ├──────────────────────────────────────┤   │
│                   │ +addError(in test : Test, in t : Throwable)      │
│                   │ +addFailure(in test : Test, in e : AssertionFailedError) │
│                   │ +endTest(in test : Test)             │   │
│                   │ +startTest(in test : Test)           │   │
│                   └──────────────────────────────────────┘   │
└─────────────────────────────────────────────────────────────┘
```

Figure B-8. The interface TestListener

Constructors

None (it's an interface).

Public Methods

void addError(Test test, Throwable t)
> Informs listener that Test produced an error.

void addFailure(Test test, AssertionFailedError e)
> Informs listener that Test produced a failure.

void endTest(Test test)
> Informs listener that Test finished.

void startTest(Test test)
> Informs listener that Test is about to be run.

Protected/Private Methods

None.

Attributes

None.

TestResult

Description

TestResult (see Figure B-9) is a class used to collect unit test results. The information collected includes a count of tests run and any failures or errors produced. Failures and errors are represented as instances of TestFailure. A TestResult runs a Test by calling its runBare( ) method.

A set of unit tests is run by creating an empty TestResult and calling run(TestResult) on each Test, passing the TestResult as a collecting parameter. At the end, the set of results is retrieved from the TestResult and reported.

A TestResult also is created when the method Test.run( ) is used to execute a Test.

Declaration

```
public class TestResult
    extends Object
```

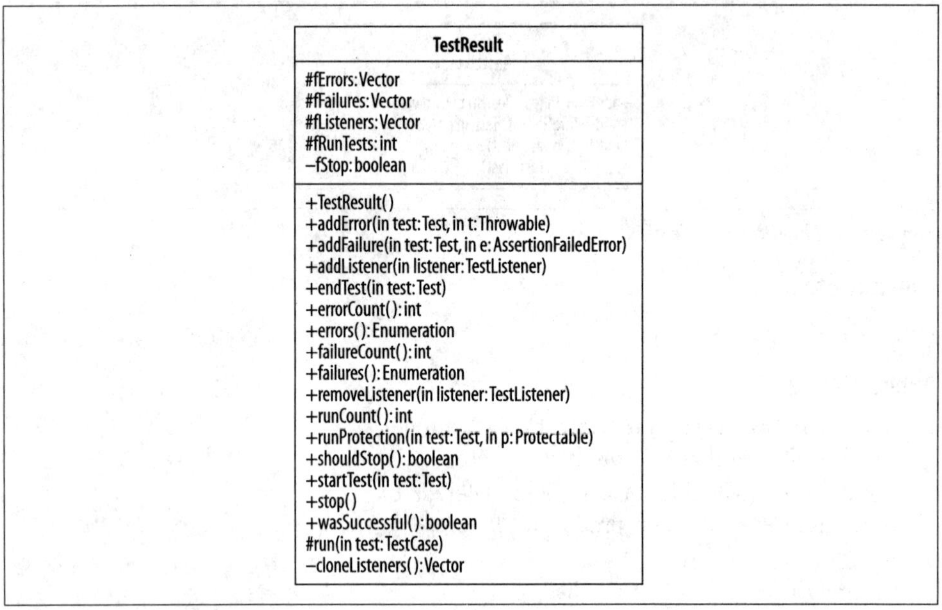

TestResult
#fErrors: Vector #fFailures: Vector #fListeners: Vector #fRunTests: int −fStop: boolean
+TestResult( ) +addError(in test: Test, in t: Throwable) +addFailure(in test: Test, in e: AssertionFailedError) +addListener(in listener: TestListener) +endTest(in test: Test) +errorCount( ): int +errors( ): Enumeration +failureCount( ): int +failures( ): Enumeration +removeListener(in listener: TestListener) +runCount( ): int +runProtection(in test: Test, In p: Protectable) +shouldStop( ): boolean +startTest(in test: Test) +stop( ) +wasSuccessful( ): boolean #run(in test: TestCase) −cloneListeners( ): Vector

Figure B-9. The class TestResult

Constructors

TestResult( )
> A constructor creating an empty TestResult.

Public Methods

void addError(Test test, Throwable t)
> Adds an error to the results.

void addFailure(Test test, AssertionFailedError e)
> Adds a failure to the results.

void addListener(TestListener listener)
> Registers a TestListener to receive events from this TestResult.

void endTest(Test test)
> Informs the listeners that Test completed.

int errorCount( )
> Gets the number of errors in the results.

Enumeration errors( )
> Gets an Enumeration of the errors.

int failureCount( )
> Gets the number of failures in the results.

Enumeration failures( )
> Gets an Enumeration of the failures.

```
void removeListener(TestListener listener)
```
Unregisters a TestListener.
```
int runCount( )
```
Gets the number of tests run.
```
void runProtected(Test test, Protectable p)
```
Runs a Protectable and associates any failures or errors with Test. The Protectable is assumed to run the Test's test method.
```
boolean shouldStop( )
```
Returns the stop flag.
```
void startTest(Test test)
```
Informs listeners that Test is starting. Also increments fRunTests by the amount returned by Test.countTestCases( ).
```
void stop( )
```
Sets the stop flag.
```
boolean wasSuccessful( )
```
Returns TRUE if there are no failures or errors in the results.

Protected/Private Methods

```
protected void run(TestCase test)
```
A method to run a TestCase.
```
private Vector cloneListeners( )
```
A method to return a copy of the listeners.

Attributes

```
protected Vector fErrors
```
A collection of TestFailures representing errors.
```
protected Vector fFailures
```
A collection of TestFailures representing failures.
```
protected Vector fListeners
```
A list of TestListeners for this TestResult.
```
protected int fRunTests
```
A counter to record the number of tests run.
```
private boolean fStop
```
A stop flag indicating that tests should stop running.

TestSuite

Description

TestSuite (see Figure B-10) is a class representing a collection of Tests. Since it implements Test, it can be run just like a TestCase. When run, a TestSuite runs all the Tests it contains. It may contain both TestCases and other TestSuites.

A TestSuite can be constructed by giving it the class name of a TestCase. The TestSuite constructor uses reflection to find all methods in the TestCase having names starting with test. The code below adds all of BookTest's test methods to a TestSuite and runs it:

```
TestSuite test = new TestSuite( BookTest.class );
test.run( new TestResult() );
```

Tests also can be added to a TestSuite using the addTest( ) method.

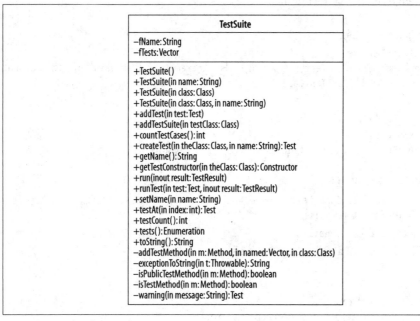

Figure B-10. The class TestSuite

Declaration

```
public class TestSuite
extends Object
implements Test
```

Constructors

TestSuite( )

A constructor that creates an empty TestSuite.

TestSuite(String name)

A constructor that creates an empty TestSuite with the given name.

TestSuite(Class class)

A constructor that takes a Class, uses reflection to find all methods with names starting with test, and adds them to the TestSuite as test methods.

TestSuite(Class class, String name)

A constructor that creates a TestSuite with the given name and all test methods found in the Class, as described for the previous constructor.

Public Methods

void addTest(Test test)
> Adds a Test to the TestSuite.

void addTestSuite(Class testClass)
> Adds the test methods from the Class to the TestSuite. Test methods are found using reflection.

int countTestCases( )
> Returns the total number of test cases that will be run by this TestSuite. Test cases are counted by recursively calling countTestCases( ) for every Test in this TestSuite.

static Test createTest(Class theClass, String name)
> Creates an instance of Class as a Test with the given name.

String getName( )
> Returns the name of the TestSuite.

static java.lang.reflect.Constructor getTestConstructor(Class theClass)
> Gets a constructor for the given Class that takes a single String as its argument, or gets a constructor that takes no arguments.

void run(TestResult result)
> Runs the Tests in this TestSuite and collects the results in TestResult.

void runTest(Test test, TestResult result)
> Runs Test and collects the results in TestResult.

void setName(String name)
> Sets the name of the TestSuite.

Test testAt(int index)
> Returns the Test at the given index.

int testCount( )
> Returns the number of Tests in this TestSuite.

java.util.Enumeration tests( )
> Returns the Tests as an Enumeration.

String toString( )
> Returns a string representation of this TestSuite.

Protected/Private Methods

private void addTestMethod(java.lang.reflect.Method m, Vector names, Class class)
> A private method to add a test method to this TestSuite.

private static String exceptionToString(Throwable t)
> Returns the Throwable's stack trace as a string.

private boolean isPublicTestMethod(java.lang.reflect.Method m)
> Returns TRUE if Method has public access.

private boolean isTestMethod(java.lang.reflect.Method m)
> A private method that returns TRUE if Method has no arguments, returns void, and has public access.

private static Test warning(String message)
> Returns a Test that will fail and logs a warning message.

Attributes

`private String fName`
> The name of this TestSuite.

`private Vector fTests`
> The Tests contained by this TestSuite.

CppUnit Class Reference

This appendix contains a detailed reference for the CppUnit classes. Knowledge of the details of CppUnit's implementation is not necessary to use it for writing and running unit tests. However, understanding the architecture is important for more advanced usage, such as developing extensions.

In the descriptions that follow, the types string, ostream, map, deque, and vector belong to the namespace std. All the header files are located under the CppUnit installation directory in *include/cppunit*. Some are located in subdirectories of this directory, such as *extensions*. All the source files are located in *src/cppunit*.

The entries are in alphabetical order by class name.

assertion_traits

Description

The template assertion_traits (see Figure C-1) is used by the CPPUNIT_ASSERT_EQUAL( ) macro. The template is specialized for different data types that are passed to the macro. For example, the template specialization assertion_traits<int> is used when CPPUNIT_ASSERT_EQUAL( ) takes arguments of type int.

The declaration of assertion_traits is found in *TestAssert.h*. It belongs to the namespace CppUnit.

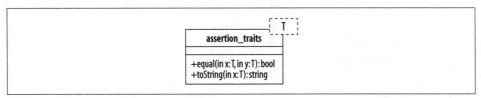

Figure C-1. The template assertion_traits

Declaration

```
template<class T> struct assertion_traits<T>
```

Constructors/Destructors

None.

Public Methods

static bool equal(const T& x, const T& y)
> A function template to compare two arguments of type T. The default implementation compares them using ==.

static string toString(const T& x)
> A function template to output a string representing the input argument of type T. The default implementation creates the output string by creating a std::OStringStream and using its << operator.

Protected/Private Methods

None.

Attributes

None.

AutoRegisterSuite

Description

The template AutoRegisterSuite (Figure C-2) is not intended for direct usage. It is statically instantiated by the macros CPPUNIT_TEST_SUITE_REGISTRATION() and CPPUNIT_TEST_SUITE_NAMED_REGISTRATION(). It registers a test of the type TestCaseType. For more details on test registration, see the description of "TestFactoryRegistry," later in this appendix.

AutoRegisterSuite belongs to the namespace CppUnit. It is declared and implemented in *extensions/AutoRegisterSuite.h*.

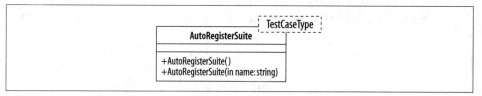

Figure C-2. The template AutoRegisterSuite

Declaration

```
template<typename TestCaseType>
    class AutoRegisterSuite<TestCaseType>
```

Constructors/Destructors

`AutoRegisterSuite( )`
> Registers the test suite in the global registry.

`AutoRegisterSuite(const string& name)`
> Registers the test suite in the registry specified by name.

Public Methods

None.

Protected/Private Methods

None.

Attributes

None.

CompilerOutputter

Description

The class `CompilerOutputter` (see Figure C-3) is a subclass of `Outputter`. It outputs test results in the format that the Microsoft Visual C++ (VC++) IDE uses for compiler errors, enabling the IDE to locate test assertions in the code.

`CompilerOutputter` belongs to the namespace `CppUnit`. It is declared in *CompilerOutputter.h* and implemented in *CompilerOutputter.cpp*.

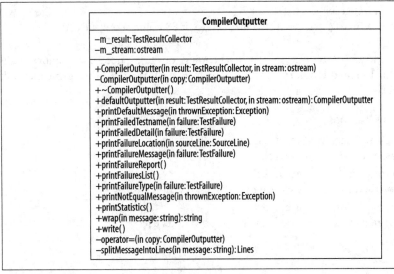

Figure C-3. The class CompilerOutputter

Declaration

```
class CompilerOutputter : public Outputter
```

Constructors/Destructors

```
CompilerOutputter(TestResultCollector *result, ostream& stream)
```
Creates a CompilerOutputter to get test results from result and outputs them to stream.

```
virtual ~CompilerOutputter( )
```
A destructor.

Public Methods

```
static CompilerOutputter *defaultOutputter( TestResultCollector *result, ostream&
stream)
```
A static method that returns a new CompilerOutputter.

```
virtual void printDefaultMessage(Exception *thrownException)
virtual void printFailedTestName(TestFailure *failure)
virtual void printFailureDetail(TestFailure *failure)
virtual void printFailureLocation(SourceLine sourceLine)
virtual void printFailureMessage(TestFailure *failure)
virtual void printFailureReport( )
virtual void printFailuresList( )
virtual void printFailureType(TestFailure *failure)
virtual void printNotEqualMessage(Exception *thrownException)
virtual void printStatistics( )
virtual void printSucess( )
```
Methods that write test results from m_result to m_stream. Called by write( ).

```
virtual string wrap(string message)
```
Returns message with carriage returns inserted to fit 80-column output width.

```
void write( )
```
A method called to output results. Depending on test success or failure, calls printSucess( ) or printFailureReport( ), which in turn call the other print methods just described.

Protected/Private Methods

```
static Lines splitMessageIntoLines(string message)
```
Breaks message into Lines (private).

```
CompilerOutputter(const CompilerOutputter& copy)
```
A copy constructor, which is scoped private to prevent its use.

```
void operator=(const CompilerOutputter& copy)
```
A copy operator, which is scoped private to prevent its use.

Attributes

typedef vector<string> Lines
    Defines the type Lines as a vector of string (private).

TestResultCollector *m_result
    The TestResultCollector passed in the constructor (private)

ostream& m_stream
    The output stream passed in the constructor (private).

Exception

Description

The class Exception (see Figure C-4) is descended from std::exception. It contains a message describing the assertion failure and a SourceLine giving its location.

Exception contains a nested class named Exception::Type. The Type value represents the named Exception type, allowing runtime Exception type identification. For the base Exception class, the Type is CppUnit::Exception.

Exception belongs to the namespace CppUnit. It is declared in *Exception.h* and implemented in *Exception.cpp*.

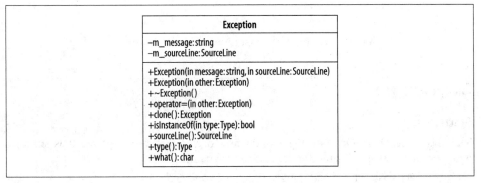

Figure C-4. *The class Exception*

Declaration

    class Exception : public std::exception

Constructors/Destructors

Exception(string message = "", SourceLine sourceLine = SourceLine())
    A constructor for Exception. The message and sourceLine arguments have default empty values.

Exception(const Exception& other)
    A copy constructor.

virtual ~Exception() throw()
    A destructor.

Public Methods

`Exception& operator=(const Exception& other)`
    A copy operator.

`virtual Exception *clone( ) const`
    Returns a copy of the Exception.

`virtual bool isInstanceOf(const Type& type) const`
    Returns TRUE if the Exception is of the given Type. Used for runtime Exception type identification.

`SourceLine sourceLine( ) const`
    Returns m_sourceLine.

`static Type type( )`
    Returns CppUnit::Exception.

`const char *what() const throw( )`
    Returns m_message as a C-style string.

Protected/Private Methods

None.

Attributes

`string m_message`
    Assertion failure message (private).

`SourceLine m_sourceLine`
    SourceLine giving the location of the assertion failure (private).

Exception::Type

Description

The class Exception::Type (see Figure C-5) nested class within Exception. It is simply a wrapper for a string containing an Exception type name.

Exception::Type is declared and implemented in *Exception.h.*

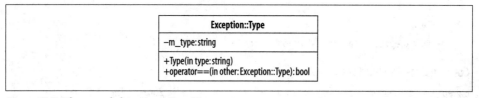

Figure C-5. The nested class Exception::Type

Declaration

    class Type

Constructors/Destructors

Type(string type)
    A constructor.

Public Methods

bool operator==(const Type& other) const
    An equality operator. Returns TRUE if this Type is equal to other.

Protected/Private Methods

None.

Attributes

const string m_type
    The Type name (private).

ExpectedExceptionTraits

Description

The template ExpectedExceptionTraits (see Figure C-6) is used by TestCaller to expect an Exception. It is an implementation detail and should not be used directly. A specialization of this template to expect that no Exception is defined:

    template<>
        struct ExpectedExceptionTraits<NoExceptionExpected>

The class NoExceptionExpected is used in this template specialization and should not be used otherwise.

ExpectedExceptionTraits belongs to the namespace CppUnit. It is declared and implemented in *TestCaller.h*.

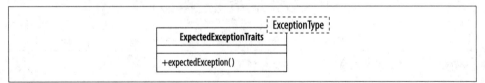

Figure C-6. The template ExpectedExceptionTraits

Declaration

    template<typename ExceptionType>
        struct ExpectedExceptionTraits<ExceptionType>

Constructors/Destructors

None.

Public Methods

`static void expectedException( )`
    A method to throw an `Exception` if the expected `Exception` is not caught.

Protected/Private Methods

None.

Attributes

None.

NamedRegistries

Description

The class `NamedRegistries` (see Figure C-7) manages all instances of `TestFactoryRegistry` and is responsible for their creation and destruction. It also keeps track of which instances of `TestFactory` have been destroyed, thus preventing multiple deletions.

`NamedRegistries` is a singleton: there is one and only one static instance of it. Thus, it has no constructor. A reference to the single `NamedRegistries` object is obtained using its static `getInstance( )` method.

`NamedRegistries` belongs to the namespace `CppUnit`. It is declared and implemented in *TestFactoryRegistry.cpp*.

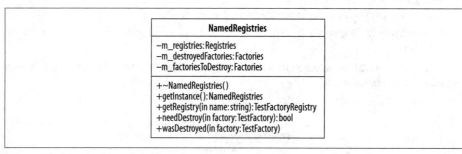

Figure C-7. The singleton class NamedRegistries

Declaration

    `class NamedRegistries`

Constructors/Destructors

`~NamedRegistries( )`
    A destructor. Deletes all instances of `TestFactoryRegistry`.

Public Methods

`static NamedRegistries& getInstance( )`
    Gets a reference to the single `NamedRegistries` object.

`TestFactoryRegistry& getRegistry(string name)`
    Returns the named `TestFactoryRegistry` if it exists; otherwise, creates a new one with the given name and returns it.

`bool needDestroy(TestFactory *factory)`
    Returns `TRUE` if factory has not yet been destroyed.

`void wasDestroyed(TestFactory *factory)`
    Signals that factory was destroyed.

Protected/Private Methods

None.

Attributes

`typedef map<string, TestFactoryRegistry*> Registries`
    Defines the type `Registries` as a map of `TestFactoryRegistry` by name (private).

`typedef std::set<TestFactory*> Factories`
    Defines the type `Factories` as a set of `TestFactory` (private).

`Registries m_registries`
    Contains managed instances of `TestFactoryRegistry` (private).

`Factories m_destroyedFactories`
    Contains instances of `TestFactory` that have been destroyed (private).

`Factories m_factoriesToDestroy`
    Contains instances of `TestFactory` that need to be destroyed (private).

NotEqualException

Description

The class `NotEqualException` (see Figure C-8) is a subclass of `Exception`. A `NotEqual-Exception` is thrown when an equality assertion fails. Its Type is `CppUnit::NotEqualException`.

`NotEqualException` belongs to the namespace `CppUnit`. It is declared in *NotEqualException.h* and implemented in *NotEqualException.cpp*.

Declaration

```
class NotEqualException : public Exception
```

```
                        NotEqualException
 −m_actual: string
 −m_additionaMessage: string
 −m_expected: string

 +NotEqualException(in expected: string, in actual: string, in sourceLine: SourceLine, inadditionalMessage: string)
 +NotEqualException(in other: NotEqualException)
 +~NotEqualException( )
 +operator=(in other: NotEqualException): NotEqualException
 +actualValue( ): string
 +additionalMessage( ): string
 +clone( ): Exception
 +expectedValue( ): string
 +isInstanceOfValue( ): string
 +type( ): Type
```

Figure C-8. The class NotEqualException

Constructors/Destructors

```
NotEqualException(string expected, string actual, SourceLine sourceLine =
    SourceLine( ), string additionalMessage = "")
```

A constructor for NotEqualException. The string arguments expected and actual represent the values that fail the equality test and cause the NotEqualException. The sourceLine and additionalMessage arguments have default empty values.

```
NotEqualException(const NotEqualException& other)
```
    A copy constructor.

```
virtual ~NotEqualException() throw( )
```
    A destructor.

Public Methods

```
NotEqualException& operator=(const NotEqualException& other)
```
    A copy operator.

```
string actualValue( ) const
```
    Returns the actual value.

```
string additionalMessage( ) const
```
    Returns the additionalMessage.

```
virtual Exception *clone( ) const
```
    Returns a copy of the NotEqualException.

```
string expectedValue( ) const
```
    Returns the expected value.

```
virtual bool isInstanceOf(const Type& type) const
```
    Returns TRUE if the NotEqualException is of the given Type. Used for runtime Exception type identification.

```
static Type type( )
```
    Returns CppUnit::NotEqualException.

Protected/Private Methods

None.

Attributes

string m_actual
    The actual value for the equality test (private).

string m_additionalMessage
    An assertion failure message (private).

string m_expected
    The expected value for the equality test (private).

Orthodox

Description

The template Orthodox (see Figure C-9) is a subclass of TestCase. When specialized for a class, it tests the class for "orthodoxy," represented by the following conditions:

- The class has a default (no argument) constructor
- The class has equality (==) and inequality (!=) operators
- The class has an assignment (=) operator
- The class has a negation (!) operator
- The class has a copy constructor

The test verifies not only that ClassUnderTest has these operations, but also that the operations' semantics are correct. For example, double negation should result in equality.

The main purpose of Orthodox is to serve as a working example of a templated test case.

Orthodox belongs to the namespace CppUnit. It is declared and implemented in *extensions/Orthodox.h*.

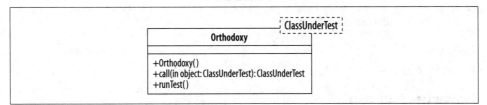

Figure C-9. The templated test class Orthodoxy

Declaration

```
template<typename ClassUnderTest>
    class Orthodox : public TestCase
```

Constructors/Destructors

Orthodox( )

A constructor.

Public Methods

`ClassUnderTest call(ClassUnderTest object)`

Returns object.

`void runTest( )`

Runs the orthodoxy tests.

Protected/Private Methods

None.

Attributes

None.

Outputter

Description

The abstract class `Outputter` (see Figure C-10) represents the interface for the output of test result summaries. It's classes re `TextOutputter`, `XmlOutputter`, it is implemented in `CompilerOutputter`.

`Outputter` belongs to the namespace `CppUnit`. It is declared in *Outputter.h*.

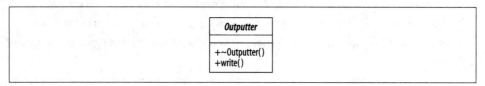

Figure C-10. The abstract class Outputter

Declaration

    class Outputter

Constructors/Destructors

`virtual ~Outputter( )`

A destructor.

Public Methods

`virtual void write( ) = 0`

A pure, virtual method representing the `Outputter` interface.

Protected/Private Methods

None.

Attributes

None.

RepeatedTest

Description

The class RepeatedTest (see Figure C-11) is a subclass of TestDecorator. It runs a Test for a specified number of repetitions.

RepeatedTest belongs to the namespace CppUnit. It is declared in *extensions/RepeatedTest.h* and implemented in *RepeatedTest.cpp*.

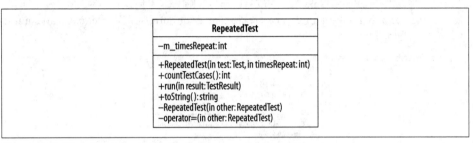

Figure C-11. The class RepeatedTest

Declaration

```
class RepeatedTest : public TestDecorator
```

Constructors/Destructors

RepeatedTest(Test *test, int timesRepeat)
: A constructor taking the Test to run and the number of repetitions.

Public Methods

int countTestCases( ) const
: Returns the number of test cases that this RepeatedTest will run, which is the number of test cases the Test contains multiplied by the number of repetitions.

void run(TestResult *result)
: A method to run the RepeatedTest.

string toString( ) const
: Returns a string representation of the RepeatedTest.

Protected/Private Methods

RepeatedTest(const RepeatedTest &)
: A copy constructor declared private to prevent its use.

void operator=(const RepeatedTest &)
: A copy operator declared private to prevent its use.

Attributes

const int m_timesRepeat
: The number of test repetitions to run (private).

SourceLine

Description

The class SourceLine (see Figure C-12) represents a location in a source code file. It is used to capture the location of an assertion failure. A SourceLine usually is created using the macro CPPUNIT_SOURCELINE(), which uses the preprocessor directives __FILE__ and __LINE__ to obtain the filename and line number of the location where it's invoked:

```
#define CPPUNIT_SOURCELINE() ::CppUnit::SourceLine( __FILE__, __LINE__ )
```

SourceLine belongs to the namespace CppUnit. It is declared in *SourceLine.h* and implemented in *SourceLine.cpp*.

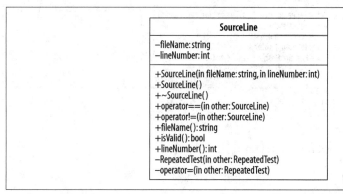

Figure C-12. The class SourceLine

Declaration

```
class SourceLine
```

Constructors/Destructors

SourceLine(string &fileName, int lineNumber)
 A constructor taking a filename and line number.

SourceLine( )
 A default constructor creating an uninitialized SourceLine.

virtual ~SourceLine( )
 A destructor.

Public Methods

bool operator==(const SourceLine &other) const
 A comparison operator.

bool operator!=(const SourceLine &other) const
 An inequality operator.

string fileName( ) const
 Returns the filename.

```
bool isValid( ) const
```
Returns TRUE if SourceLine is initialized (the filename is not empty).
```
int lineNumber( ) const
```
Returns the line number.

Protected/Private Methods

```
RepeatedTest(const RepeatedTest &)
```
A copy constructor declared private to prevent its use.
```
void operator=(const RepeatedTest &)
```
A copy operator declared private to prevent its use.

Attributes

```
string m_fileName
```
The source filename (private).
```
int m_lineNumber
```
The source file line number (private).

SynchronizedObject

Description

The class SynchronizedObject (see Figure C-13) serves as the parent class for synchronized objects. *Synchronized objects* incorporate a mutex-based lock mechanism, allowing them to be used concurrently by multiple threads.

SynchronizedObject includes the nested classes SynchronizationObject, which is its mutex object, and ExclusiveZone, which locks a SynchronizationObject.

SynchronizedObject belongs to the namespace CppUnit. It is declared in *SynchronizedObject.h* and implemented in *SynchronizedObject.cpp*.

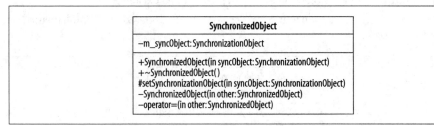

Figure C-13. The base class SynchronizedObject

Declaration

```
class SynchronizedObject
```

Constructors/Destructors

SynchronizedObject(SynchronizationObject *syncObject = 0)
> A constructor taking a SynchronizationObject (mutex.) If syncObject is null, a new SynchronizationObject is created.

virtual ~SynchronizedObject( )
> A destructor.

Public Methods

None.

Protected/Private Methods

virtual void setSynchronizationObject(SynchronizationObject *syncObject)
> Sets the SynchronizationObject.

SynchronizedObject(const SynchronizedObject &copy)
> A copy constructor declared private to prevent its use.

void operator=(const SynchronizedObject &copy)
> A copy operator declared private to prevent its use.

Attributes

SynchronizationObject *m_syncObject
> A pointer to the SynchronizationObject for this SynchronizedObject (protected).

SynchronizedObject::ExclusiveZone

Description

The class ExclusiveZone (see Figure C-14) is a nested class belonging to Synchronized-Object. It locks a SynchronizationObject (mutex) upon construction and unlocks it upon destruction, thus providing protection during the scope of its existence.

ExclusiveZone belongs to the namespace CppUnit. It is declared and implemented in *SynchronizedObject.h*.

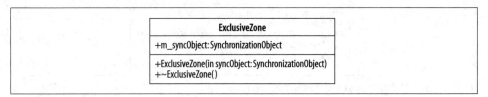

Figure C-14. The nested class SynchronizedObject::ExclusiveZone

Declaration

    class ExclusiveZone

Constructors/Destructors

ExclusiveZone(SynchronizationObject *syncObject)
    Constructs ExclusiveZone and locks syncObject.

~ExclusiveZone( )
    Destroys ExclusiveZone and unlocks syncObject.

Public Methods

None.

Protected/Private Methods

None.

Attributes

SynchronizationObject *m_syncObject
    A pointer to the SynchronizationObject for this ExclusiveZone (public).

SynchronizedObject::SynchronizationObject

Description

The class SynchronizationObject (see Figure C-15) is a nested class belonging to SynchronizedObject. It acts as the mutex for a SynchronizedObject and so can be locked or unlocked.

SynchronizationObject belongs to the namespace CppUnit. It is declared and implemented in *SynchronizedObject.h*.

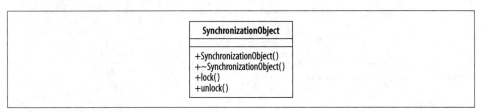

Figure C-15. The nested class SynchronizationObject

Declaration

    class SynchronizationObject

Constructors/Destructors

SynchronizationObject( )
    A constructor.

~SynchronizationObject( )
    A destructor.

Public Methods

`virtual void lock( )`
    Locks the `SynchronizationObject`.
`virtual void unlock( )`
    Unlocks the `SynchronizationObject`.

Protected/Private Methods

None.

Attributes

None.

Test

Description

The abstract class `Test` (see Figure C-16) is the central design element of CppUnit, as in other versions of xUnit. It is the base class for all test objects. A `Test` may consist of a single unit test or of a collection of `Test`s. When a `Test` is run, a `TestResult` collects its results.

All of `Test`'s methods are virtual and should be overridden by descendant classes.

`Test` belongs to the namespace `CppUnit`. It is declared in *Test.h* and implemented in *Test.cpp*.

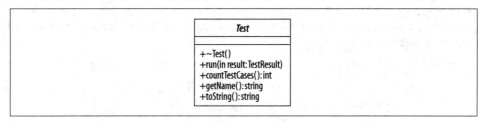

Figure C-16. *The abstract class Test*

Declaration

    `class Test`

Constructors/Destructors

`virtual ~Test( )`
    A destructor.

Public Methods

`virtual int countTestCases( ) const = 0`
    Returns the number of test cases to be run by this `Test`.
`virtual string getName( ) const = 0`
    Returns the name of this `Test`.

```
virtual void run(TestResult *result) = 0
```
    Runs Test and collects the results in result.

```
virtual string toString( ) const = 0
```
    Returns a short description of this Test, generally incorporating the name and Test type.

Protected/Private Methods

None.

Attributes

None.

TestCaller

Description

The template class TestCaller (see Figure C-17) is used to create and run a TestCase containing a TestMethod, usually in the context of a TestFixture. This is useful when a TestFixture has multiple test methods but only one of them should be run, or when test methods are being run by name. A TestMethod must take no arguments and return void to be invoked using TestCaller.

When TestCaller is specialized and instantiated, the type Fixture should be TestFixture or a subclass of it. The type ExpectedException defaults to NoExceptionExpected, meaning that an Exception is not expected when the TestMethod is run, and the test fails if one is thrown. An Exception type can be provided when TestCaller is specialized, so that it is expected when the TestCase is run. In this case, the test fails if the ExpectedException is not thrown.

TestCaller belongs to the namespace CppUnit. It is declared and implemented in *TestCaller.h*.

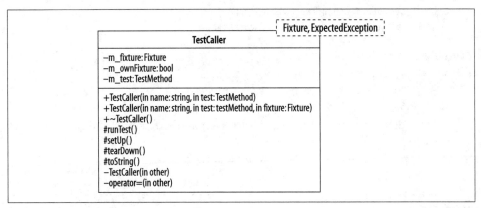

Figure C-17. The template class TestCaller

Declaration

```
template<typename Fixture, typename ExpectedException = NoExceptionExpected>
    class TestCaller : public TestCase
```

Constructors/Destructors

`TestCaller(string name, TestMethod test)`
> A constructor used when a `TestFixture` is not provided. In this case, the `TestMethod` is run in a new, default `TestFixture` owned by the `TestCaller`.

`TestCaller(string name, TestMethod test, Fixture& fixture)`
> A constructor taking a `TestMethod` and a reference to a `TestFixture`. The `TestCaller` does not own the `TestFixture` in this case.

`TestCaller(string name, TestMethod test, Fixture *fixture)`
> A constructor taking a `TestMethod` and a pointer to a `TestFixture`. When a `TestCaller` is constructed this way, it owns the `TestFixture`.

`~TestCaller()`
> A destructor. If the `TestCaller` owns the `TestFixture`, it deletes it.

Public Methods

None.

Protected/Private Methods

`void runTest()`
> A Protected method that runs the `TestMethod`.

`void setUp()`
> A Protected method that sets up the `Fixture` by calling its `setUp()` method.

`void tearDown()`
> A Protected method that tears down the `Fixture` by calling its `tearDown()` method.

`string toString() const`
> A Protected method returning a string representation of this `TestCaller`.

`TestCaller(const TestCaller &other)`
> A copy constructor declared private to prevent its use.

`TestCaller& operator=(const TestCaller &other)`
> A copy operator declared private to prevent its use.

Attributes

`Fixture *m_fixture`
> A pointer to `Fixture` (private).

`bool m_ownFixture`
> If TRUE, `TestCaller` owns `Fixture` and deletes it in its destructor (private).

`TestMethod m_test`
> The `TestMethod` that this `TestCaller` will run (private).

TestCase

Description

The class `TestCase` (see Figure C-18) represents a test object. Its purpose is to run test methods and thereby produce test results.

TestCase may be used in a number of ways. The simplest way to write a test object is to create a subclass of TestCase that overrides runTest( ) with a custom test method. To run the test object, call the run( ) method, which returns a TestResult.

More commonly, a subclass of TestFixture is created with multiple test methods. TestRunner then uses TestCaller to run the test methods, creating a new instance of TestCase for each one.

TestCase belongs to the namespace CppUnit. It is declared in *TestCase.h* and implemented in *TestCase.cpp*.

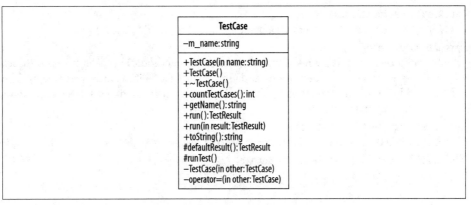

Figure C-18. The class TestCase, base class for all test objects

Declaration

```
class TestCase : public Test, public TestFixture
```

Constructors/Destructors

TestCase(string name)
> Constructs a TestCase with the given name.

TestCase( )
> The default constructor used by TestCaller to create a temporary TestCase. Should not be used directly, since it creates a TestCase with no name.

~TestCase( )
> A destructor.

Public Methods

virtual int countTestCases( ) const
> Returns 1, the number of test cases contained in a base TestCase. Descendants of TestCase may contain multiple test cases.

string getName( ) const
> Returns the TestCase name.

virtual TestResult *run( )
> A convenience method that runs this TestCase and returns a new TestResult containing the results.

```
virtual void run(TestResult *result)
```
A method that runs the test, catches any failures or errors, and collects the results in result. The sequence of calls is: setUp( ), runTest( ), tearDown( ). This method is the interface that the framework normally uses to run tests.

```
string toString( ) const
```
Returns a string representation of this TestCase, including the class name and TestCase name.

Protected/Private Methods

```
TestResult *defaultResult( )
```
A Protected method that returns a default empty TestResult. Used by run( ).

```
virtual void runTest( )
```
A Protected method representing the actual test method. The default version does nothing. May be overridden by descendants of TestCase to implement actual tests. The overridden runTest( ) method contains the test assertions that result in success or failure of the unit test.

```
TestCase(const TestCase &other)
```
A copy constructor declared private to prevent its use.

```
TestCase& operator=(const TestCase &other)
```
A copy operator declared private to prevent its use.

Attributes

```
const string m_name
```
The TestCase name (private).

TestDecorator

Description

The class TestDecorator (see Figure C-19) allows the functionality of a Test to be extended without subclassing it. TestDecorator implements the Test interface and thus can be run like any other Test. When constructed, it takes a reference to another Test that it "decorates," or wraps. A TestDecorator modifies the decorated Test by performing other operations before or after running it.

The classes RepeatedTest and TestSetUp are subclasses of TestDecorator and provide practical examples of its usage. The base implementation of TestDecorator simply is a wrapper for a Test and does not change its operation.

TestDecorator belongs to the namespace CppUnit. It is declared and implemented in *extensions/TestDecorator.h*.

Declaration

```
class TestDecorator : public Test
```

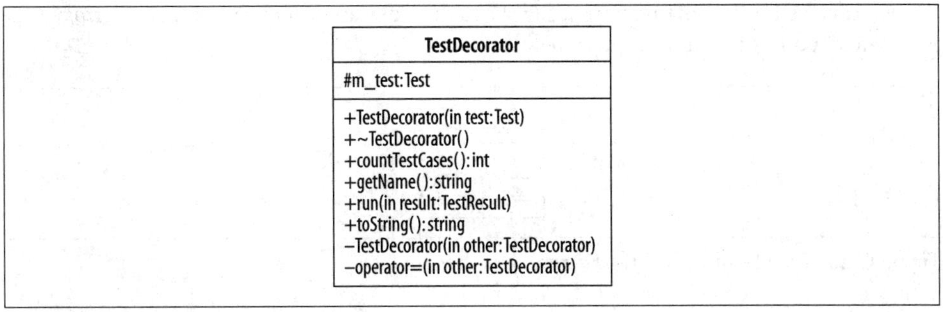

TestDecorator
#m_test:Test
+TestDecorator(in test:Test) +~TestDecorator( ) +countTestCases( ):int +getName( ):string +run(in result:TestResult) +toString( ):string −TestDecorator(in other:TestDecorator) −operator=(in other:TestDecorator)

Figure C-19. The class TestDecorator

Constructors/Destructors

TestDecorator(Test *test)
>   Constructs a TestDecorator to decorate test.

~TestDecorator( )
>   A destructor. Does not delete the decorated Test.

Public Methods

int countTestCases( ) const
>   Returns the value of countTestCases( ) for the decorated Test.

string getName( ) const
>   Returns the name of the decorated Test.

void run(TestResult *result)
>   Calls run(result) on the decorated Test.

string toString( ) const
>   Returns the value of toString( ) for the decorated Test.

Protected/Private Methods

TestDecorator(const TestDecorator &other)
>   A copy constructor declared private to prevent its use.

void operator=(const TestDecorator &other)
>   A copy operator declared private to prevent its use.

Attributes

Test *m_test
>   The Test decorated by this TestDecorator (protected).

TestFactory

Description

The abstract class TestFactory (see Figure C-20) defines the interface for a factory that produces Test objects.

TestFactory belongs to the namespace CppUnit. It is declared in *extensions/TestFactory.h*. It is abstract and has no implementation.

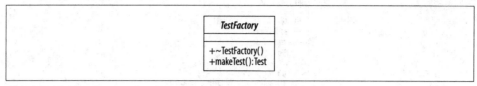

Figure C-20. The abstract class TestFactory

Declaration

    class TestFactory

Constructors/Destructors

virtual ~TestFactory( )
    A destructor.

Public Methods

virtual Test* makeTest( ) = 0
    A pure, virtual method to create a Test.

Protected/Private Methods

None.

Attributes

None.

TestFactoryRegistry

Description

The class TestFactoryRegistry (see Figure C-21) is a subclass of TestFactory. It acts as both a registry and a factory for Test objects. It registers Tests, and it produces TestSuites containing registered Tests. Rather than containing the registered Test objects themselves, it contains a TestFactory for each one.

The default registry is a TestFactoryRegistry named "All Tests." Named instances of TestFactoryRegistry may also be created.

The macro CPPUNIT_TEST_SUITE_REGISTRATION( ) takes a Test and adds a TestFactory for it to the default registry. The macro CPPUNIT_TEST_SUITE_NAMED_REGISTRATION( ) similarly adds a TestFactory to a named registry. Calling a registry's makeTest( ) method creates a TestSuite containing all the registered Tests, demonstrating the main usefulness of TestFactoryRegistry.

The singleton NamedRegistries manages all instances of TestFactoryRegistry.

The following code snippet registers the Test class BookTest in the default registry and creates a TestSuite containing it:

```
CPPUNIT_TEST_SUITE_REGISTRATION( BookTest );
TestFactoryRegistry &registry = TestFactoryRegistry::getRegistry( );
TestSuite *suite = registry.makeTest( );
```

TestFactoryRegistry belongs to the namespace CppUnit. It is declared in *extensions/ TestFactoryRegistry.h* and implemented in *TestFactoryRegistry.cpp*.

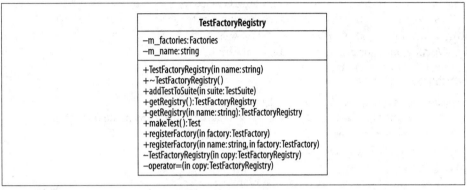

Figure C-21. The class TestFactoryRegistry

Declaration

```
class TestFactoryRegistry : public TestFactory
```

Constructors/Destructors

TestFactoryRegistry(string name = "All Tests")
> A constructor. If no name is provided, a default registry named "All Tests" is created.

virtual ~TestFactoryRegistry( )
> A destructor. Each TestFactory contained by this TestFactoryRegistry is deleted if NamedRegistries indicates that it has not already been deleted. This prevents double deletion of a TestFactory.

Public Methods

void addTestToSuite(TestSuite *suite)
> Adds the registered Test objects to a preexisting TestSuite.

static TestFactoryRegistry &getRegistry( )
> Returns the default TestFactoryRegistry named "All Tests."

static TestFactoryRegistry &getRegistry(const string &name)
> Returns a TestFactoryRegistry with the given name. If the registry doesn't already exist, it is created.

virtual Test* makeTest( )
> Creates a TestSuite containing the registered Test objects. The TestSuite has the same name as the TestFactoryRegistry. For example, the TestSuite created by the default registry is named "All Tests."

```
void registerFactory(TestFactory *factory)
```
Adds a TestFactory to the TestFactoryRegistry.
```
void registerFactory(const string &name, TestFactory *factory)
```
A deprecated method that adds a TestFactory to the TestFactoryRegistry with the given name. The previous version of registerFactory( ) should be used instead.

Protected/Private Methods

```
TestFactoryRegistry(const TestFactoryRegistry &copy)
```
A copy constructor declared private to prevent its use.
```
void operator=(const TestFactoryRegistry &copy)
```
A copy operator declared private to prevent its use.

Attributes

```
typedef map<string, TestFactory *> Factories
```
Defines the type Factories as a map of TestFactory objects by name (private).
```
Factories m_factories
```
```
Registered TestFactory objects (private).
string m_name
```
The name of this TestFactoryRegistry (private).

TestFailure

Description

The class TestFailure (see Figure C-22) summarizes the failure of a Test. The failure may be due to an assertion failure or an error. An error is defined as any exception that isn't an assertion failure.

TestFailure belongs to the namespace CppUnit. It is declared in *TestFailure.h* and is implemented in *TestFailure.cpp*.

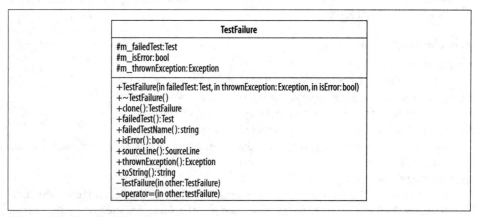

Figure C-22. The class TestFailure

Declaration

```
class TestFailure
```

Constructors/Destructors

```
TestFailure(Test *failedTest, Exception *thrownException, bool isError)
```
A constructor taking the Test that failed, the Exception that was thrown, and a flag indicating whether the failure was an assertion failure or an error.

```
virtual ~TestFailure()
```
A destructor.

Public Methods

```
virtual TestFailure *clone() const
```
Returns a copy of this TestFailure.

```
virtual Test *failedTest() const
```
Returns the failed Test.

```
virtual string failedTestName() const
```
Returns the name of the failed Test.

```
virtual bool isError() const
```
Returns TRUE if the TestFailure is due to an error and not to an assertion failure.

```
virtual SourceLine sourceLine() const
```
Returns the SourceLine for this TestFailure.

```
virtual Exception *thrownException() const
```
Returns the Exception associated with this TestFailure.

```
virtual string toString() const
```
Returns a string representation of this TestFailure.

Protected/Private Methods

```
TestFailure(const TestFailure &other)
```
A copy constructor declared private to prevent its use.

```
TestFailure& operator=(const TestFailure& other)
```
A copy operator declared private to prevent its use.

Attributes

```
Test *m_failedTest
```
The failed Test (protected).

```
bool m_isError
```
Returns TRUE if the TestFailure is due to an error, FALSE if it is due to an assertion failure (protected).

```
Exception *m_thrownException
```
The Exception associated with this TestFailure (protected).

TestFixture

Description

The class `TestFixture` (see Figure C-23) defines the interface of a test fixture. `TestCase` is descended from `TestFixture`, so every test object is implicitly a test fixture. However, a test object is truly being used as a fixture only if it has multiple test methods that share objects. Philosophically, a fixture is a test environment, and the test methods interact with the environment to test different behaviors.

The `TestFixture` methods `setUp()` and `tearDown()` are used to initialize and clean up the fixture's shared objects. When there are multiple test methods in the fixture, `setUp()` and `tearDown()` are called for each one. This ensures test isolation by making sure the fixture is in the same state for each test.

`TestFixture` belongs to the namespace `CppUnit`. It is declared and implemented in *TestFixture.h*.

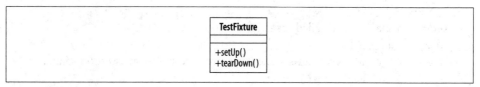

Figure C-23. The class TestFixture

Declaration

    class TestFixture

Constructors/Destructors

`virtual ~TestFixture()`
A destructor.

Public Methods

`virtual void setUp() {}`
Initializes the fixture's shared objects. The default implementation does nothing.
`virtual void tearDown() {}`
Cleans up the fixture's shared objects. The default implementation does nothing.

Protected/Private Methods

None.

Attributes

None.

TestFixtureFactory

Description

The abstract class TestFixtureFactory (see Figure C-24) defines the interface for a factory to produce TestFixture objects.

TestFixtureFactory belongs to the namespace CppUnit. It is declared in *extensions/HelperMacros.h*. It is abstract and has no implementation.

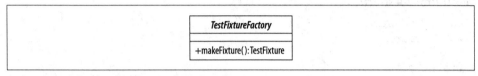

Figure C-24. The abstract class TestFixtureFactory

Declaration

```
class TestFixtureFactory
```

Constructors/Destructors

None.

Public Methods

virtual TestFixture *makeFixture( ) = 0
  A pure virtual method to create a TestFixture.

Protected/Private Methods

None.

Attributes

None.

TestListener

Description

The class TestListener (see Figure C-25) defines an interface for observers to receive test progress notifications from a TestResult. The method TestResult::addListener( ) is used to register a TestListener.

TestListener belongs to the namespace CppUnit. It is declared in *TestListener.h*, which also provides its default empty implementation.

Declaration

```
class TestListener
```

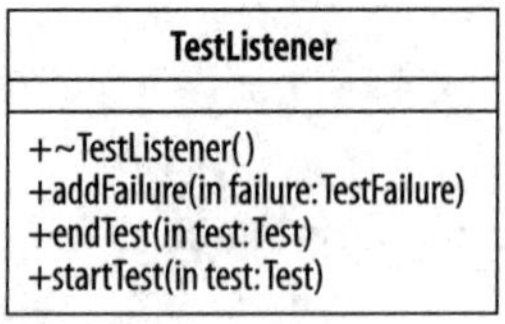

TestListener
+~TestListener( )
+addFailure(in failure:TestFailure)
+endTest(in test:Test)
+startTest(in test:Test)

Figure C-25. The class TestListener

Constructors/Destructors

```
virtual ~TestListener( )
```
   A destructor.

Public Methods

```
virtual void addFailure(const TestFailure &failure)
```
   A method called to notify the TestListener that a failure has occurred. The argument
   failure is a temporary object that is deleted after the call.

```
virtual void endTest(Test *test)
```
   A method called to notify the TestListener that test has ended.

```
virtual void startTest(Test *test)
```
   A method called to notify the TestListener that test is about to be run.

Protected/Private Methods

None.

Attributes

None.

TestResult

Description

The class TestResult (see Figure C-26) receives test results from Test objects. Test results
can be categorized as successes, failures, and errors. Normally, when multiple Test classes
are run, a single TestResult is passed to the run( ) method of each Test.

A TestResult informs its observers of test progress and results using the TestListener interface. The TestListener subclass TestResultCollector normally is used to store the results.
TestResult doesn't store the results itself.

A TestResult is a SynchronizedObject. Its operations are mutex-protected and thread-safe,
allowing Test and TestListener objects to run in separate threads.

TestResult belongs to the namespace CppUnit. It is declared in *TestResult.h* and implemented in *TestResult.cpp*.

Declaration

```
class TestResult : protected SynchronizedObject
```

```
                    ┌─────────────────────────────────────────────────┐
                    │                   TestResult                     │
                    ├─────────────────────────────────────────────────┤
                    │ #m_listeners: TestListeners                      │
                    │ #m_stop: bool                                    │
                    ├─────────────────────────────────────────────────┤
                    │ +TestResult(in syncObject: SynchronizationObject)│
                    │ +~TestResult()                                   │
                    │ +addError(in test: Test, in e: Exception)        │
                    │ +addFailure(in test: Test, in e: Exception)      │
                    │ +addListener(in listener: TestListener)          │
                    │ +endTest(in test: Test)                          │
                    │ +removeListener(in listener: TestListener)       │
                    │ +reset()                                         │
                    │ +shouldStop(): bool                              │
                    │ +startTest(in test: Test)                        │
                    │ +stop()                                          │
                    │ #addFailure(in failure: TestFailure)             │
                    │ −TestResult(in other: TestResult)                │
                    │ −operator=(in other: TestResult)                 │
                    └─────────────────────────────────────────────────┘
```

Figure C-26. The class TestResult

Constructors/Destructors

TestResult(SynchronizationObject *syncObject = 0)

> A constructor. If a SynchronizationObject is not provided, a new one is created.

virtual ~TestResult( )

> A destructor.

Public Methods

virtual void addError(Test *test, Exception *e)

> A method that informs TestResult of a test error (an Exception not caused by a test assertion).

virtual void addFailure(Test *test, Exception *e)

> A method that informs TestResult of a test failure (an Exception caused by a test assertion).

virtual void addListener(TestListener *listener)

> Adds a TestListener to this TestResult.

virtual void endTest(Test *test)

> A method that informs TestResult that test has ended.

virtual void removeListener(TestListener *listener)

> Removes a TestListener from this TestResult.

virtual void reset( )

> Sets m_stop to FALSE to prepare for a new test run.

virtual bool shouldStop( ) const

> Returns the value of m_stop.

virtual void startTest(Test *test)

> A method that informs TestResult that test is about to be run.

virtual void stop( )

> Sets m_stop to TRUE to stop the test run.

Protected/Private Methods

`void addFailure(const TestFailure &failure)`
> A protected method that adds a `TestFailure` and inform listeners.

`TestResult(const TestResult &other)`
> A copy constructor declared private to prevent its use.

`TestResult& operator=(const TestResult &other)`
> A copy operator declared private to prevent its use.

Attributes

`typedef deque<TestListener *> TestListeners`
> Defines the type `TestListeners` as a deque of `TestListener` objects (protected).

`TestListeners m_listeners`
> The test listeners (protected).

`bool m_stop`
> If `TRUE`, the test run should stop (protected).

TestResultCollector

Description

The class `TestResultCollector` (see Figure C-27) collects test results that it receives from a `TestResult` via the `TestListener` interface. The results consist of the Test objects run and any failures or errors produced.

A `TestResultCollector` is a `SynchronizedObject`. Its operations are mutex-protected and thread-safe.

`TestResultCollector` belongs to the namespace `CppUnit`. It is declared in *TestResult-Collector.h* and implemented in *TestResultCollector.cpp*.

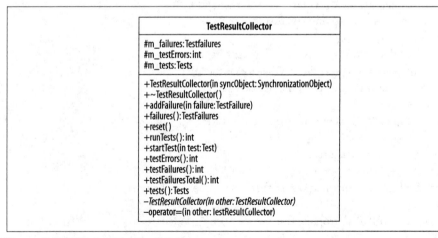

Figure C-27. The class TestResultCollector

Declaration

```
class TestResultCollector : public TestSucessListener
```

Constructors/Destructors

```
TestResultCollector(SynchronizationObject *syncObject = 0)
```
A constructor. If a SynchronizationObject is not provided, a new one is created.

```
virtual ~TestResultCollector( )
```
A destructor.

Public Methods

```
void addFailure(const TestFailure &failure)
```
A method that informs TestResultCollector of a TestFailure.

```
virtual const TestFailures& failures( ) const
```
Returns m_failures, the TestFailure objects collected by this TestResultCollector.

```
virtual void reset( )
```
Clears the collected results.

```
virtual int runTests( ) const
```
Returns the number of Test objects run.

```
void startTest(Test *test)
```
A method that informs TestResultCollector that test is about to be run.

```
virtual int testErrors( ) const
```
Returns the number of test errors collected.

```
virtual int testFailures( ) const
```
Returns the number of test failures collected.

```
virtual int testFailuresTotal( ) const
```
Returns the total number of test failures and errors collected.

```
virtual const Tests &tests( ) const
```
Returns m_tests, the Test objects collected by this TestResultCollector.

Protected/Private Methods

```
TestResultCollector(const TestResultCollector &other)
```
A copy constructor declared private to prevent its use.

```
TestResultCollector& operator=(const TestResultCollector &other)
```
A copy operator declared private to prevent its use.

Attributes

```
typedef deque<TestFailure *> TestFailures
```
Defines the type TestFailures as a deque of TestFailure objects (public).

```
typedef deque<Test *> Tests
```
Defines the type Tests as a deque of Test objects (public).

```
TestFailures m_failures
    The collected failures (protected).
int m_testErrors
    The number of errors (protected).
Tests m_tests
    The collected Test objects (protected).
```

TestRunner

Description

The class TestRunner (see Figure C-28) provides the user interface to run tests and output the results. CppUnit includes three versions of TestRunner: a text version, a Qt GUI version, and an MFC GUI version. The text version is summarized here, since it is the most generic. The usage of the other two versions is similar.

The code sample below demonstrates using TestRunner to run BookTest and print the results. A TestSuite containing multiple Test objects can be run the same way.

```
TestRunner runner;
runner.addTest( BookTest );
runner.run();
```

The text TestRunner belongs to the namespace CppUnit::TextUi. It is declared in the file *ui/text/TestRunner.h* and implemented in the file *TestRunner.cpp*.

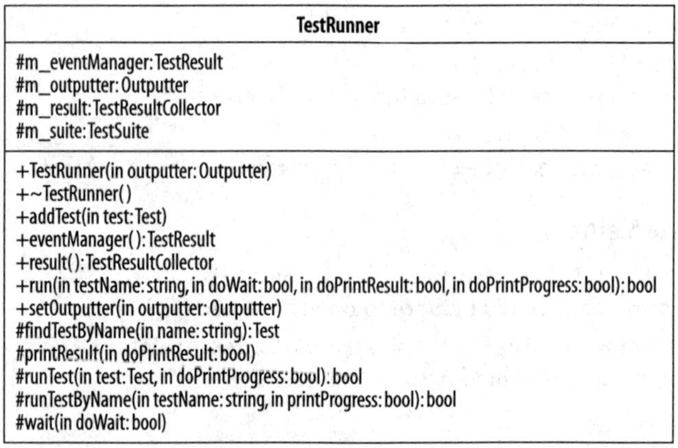

TestRunner
#m_eventManager: TestResult #m_outputter: Outputter #m_result: TestResultCollector #m_suite: TestSuite
+TestRunner(in outputter: Outputter) +~TestRunner( ) +addTest(in test: Test) +eventManager( ): TestResult +result( ): TestResultCollector +run(in testName: string, in doWait: bool, in doPrintResult: bool, in doPrintProgress: bool): bool +setOutputter(in outputter: Outputter) #findTestByName(in name: string): Test #printResult(in doPrintResult: bool) #runTest(in test: Test, in doPrintProgress: bool): bool #runTestByName(in testName: string, in printProgress: bool): bool #wait(in doWait: bool)

Figure C-28. The text version of TestRunner

Declaration

```
class TestRunner
```

Constructors/Destructors

TestRunner(Outputter *outputter = NULL)

Constructs a TestRunner. If no Outputter is provided, a TextOutputter that prints to stdout is created.

virtual ~TestRunner( )

A destructor.

Public Methods

void addTest(Test *test)

Adds a Test to this TestRunner. Multiple Test objects may be added.

TestResult &eventManager( ) const

Returns the TestResult for this TestRunner. Additional TestListener objects can be added to the TestResult to obtain test progress and results notifications.

TestResultCollector &result( ) const

Returns the TestResultCollector containing the results of the Test objects that were run.

bool run(string testName = "", bool doWait = false, bool doPrintResult = true, bool doPrintProgress = true)

Runs the Test specified by testName. If no testName is given, runs all the added Test objects. If doWait is TRUE, the user must press Return to start the run. If doPrintResult is TRUE, the test result summary is printed. If doPrintProgress is TRUE, a progress indicator is printed as the tests are run.

void setOutputter(Outputter *outputter)

Sets the Outputter object. Allows a custom Outputter to be used to output test results. The default Outputter is a TextOutputter.

Protected/Private Methods

virtual Test *findTestByName(string name) const

A protected method returning the Test with the given name, or NULL if it is not found.

virtual void printResult(bool doPrintResult)

A protected method that calls the Outputter's write( ) method if doPrintResult is TRUE.

virtual bool runTest(Test *test, bool doPrintProgress)

A protected method that runs a Test. If doPrintProgress is TRUE, a TextTest-ProgressListener is used to print a progress indicator.

virtual bool runTestByName(string testName, bool printProgress)

A protected method that calls findTestByName( ) to get the named Test and calls runTest( ) to run to run the named Test.

virtual void wait(bool doWait)

A pprotected method that waits for user input if doWait is TRUE.

Attributes

TestResult *m_eventManager
> The TestResult that receives the results of Test objects run by this TestRunner (protected).

Outputter *m_outputter
> The Outputter that outputs test results for this TestRunner (protected).

TestResultCollector *m_result
> The TestResultCollector where the test results for this TestRunner are stored (protected).

TestSuite *m_suite
> The TestSuite to which addTest( ) adds Test objects (protected).

TestSetUp

Description

The class TestSetUp (see Figure C-29) is a subclass of TestDecorator that implements setUp( ) and tearDown( ) methods for the decorated Test. This allows the Test object's test fixture behavior to be modified without subclassing it.

TestSetUp belongs to the namespace CppUnit. It is declared in the file *extensions/TestSetUp.h* and implemented in the file *TestSetUp.cpp*.

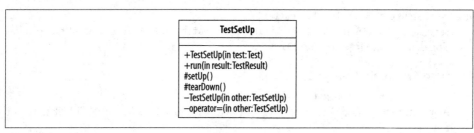

Figure C-29. The class TestSetUp

Declaration

```
class TestSetUp : public TestDecorator
```

Constructors/Destructors

TestSetUp(Test *test)
> A constructor taking the Test to decorate.

Public Methods

void run(TestResult *result)
> Calls setUp( ), runs the decorated Test, and calls tearDown( ).

Protected/Private Methods

virtual void setUp( )
> A Protected method called prior to running the decorated Test, allowing custom test fixture behavior to be implemented.

virtual void tearDown( )
> A Protected method called after running the decorated Test, allowing the test fixture to be cleaned up.

TestSetUp(const TestSetUp &)
> A copy constructor declared private to prevent its use.

void operator=(const TestSetUp &)
> A copy operator declared private to prevent its use.

Attributes

None.

TestSucessListener

Description

The class TestSucessListener (see Figure C-30) is a subclass of TestListener and SynchronizedObject. It indicates whether the Test it observes has succeeded. If the TestResult includes a failure, the Test is not successful.

TestSucessListener belongs to the namespace CppUnit. It is declared in the file *TestSucessListener.h* and implemented in the file *TestSucessListener.cpp*.

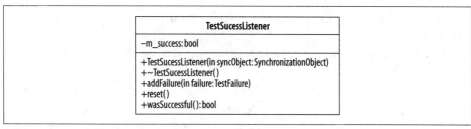

Figure C-30. The class TestSucessListener

Declaration

```
class TestSucessListener : public TestListener, public SynchronizedObject
```

Constructors/Destructors

TestSucessListener(SynchronizationObject *syncObject = 0)
> A constructor. If syncObject is null, a new SynchronizationObject is created.

virtual ~TestSucessListener( )
> A destructor.

Public Methods

void addFailure(const TestFailure &failure)
> A method to report a TestFailure to the TestSucessListener. Sets m_sucess to FALSE.

virtual void reset( )
> Resets m_sucess to TRUE.

virtual bool wasSuccessful( ) const
> Returns value of m_sucess.

Protected/Private Methods

None.

Attributes

bool m_sucess
> A test success indicator; TRUE unless there is a failure (private).

TestSuite

Description

The class TestSuite (see Figure C-31) implements the interface Test. It is a composite of Test objects. Since the contained Test objects may be instances of TestCase, TestSuite, or any other subclass of Test, this allows hierarchies of Test classes to be assembled and run as a unit. A TestSuite is run just like a TestCase: by calling its run( ) method and passing in a TestResult to receive the results. The TestSuite then sequentially runs the Test objects it contains.

A TestSuite takes ownership of all Test objects added to it and deletes them in its destructor.

TestSuite belongs to the namespace CppUnit. It is declared in the file *TestSuite.h* and implemented in the file *TestSuite.cpp*.

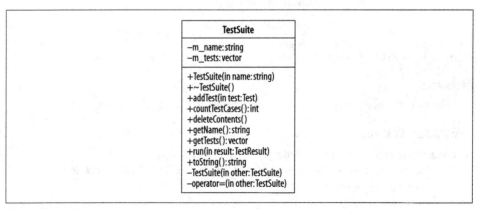

Figure C-31. The class TestSuite

Declaration

```
class TestSuite : public Test
```

Constructors/Destructors

```
TestSuite(string name = "")
```
Constructs a TestSuite, optionally giving it a name.

```
virtual ~TestSuite( )
```
A destructor. Deletes all the contained Test objects.

Public Methods

```
void addTest(Test *test)
```
Adds a Test to this TestSuite.

```
int countTestCases( ) const
```
Returns the total number of TestCase objects to be run by this TestSuite, by recursively calling countTestCases( ) on all the contained Test objects.

```
virtual void deleteContents( )
```
Deletes all the contained Test objects.

```
string getName( ) const
```
Returns the name of this TestSuite.

```
const vector<Test *> &getTests( ) const
```
Returns the collection of contained Test objects.

```
void run(TestResult *result)
```
Runs the Test objects and receives the results in result.

```
string toString( ) const
```
Returns a string representation of this TestSuite.

Protected/Private Methods

```
TestSuite(const TestSuite &other)
```
A copy constructor declared private to prevent its use.

```
TestSuite& operator=(const TestSuite &other)
```
A copy operator declared private to prevent its use.

Attributes

```
const string m_name
```
The name of this TestSuite. May be empty (private).

```
vector<Test *> m_tests
```
The collection of Test objects belonging to this TestSuite (private).

TestSuiteBuilder

Description

The template class TestSuiteBuilder (see Figure C-32) is a helper class used to add tests to a TestSuite. It is used by the macros CPPUNIT_TEST_SUITE( ) and CPPUNIT_TEST_SUITE_END( ).

TestSuiteBuilder belongs to the namespace CppUnit. It is declared and implemented in the file *extensions/TestSuiteBuilder.h*.

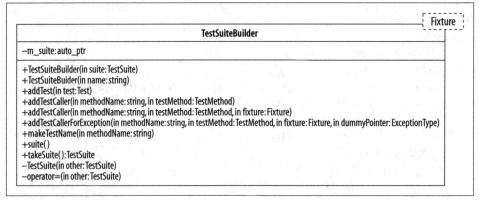

Figure C-32. The template class TestSuiteBuilder

Declaration

    template<typename Fixture> class TestSuiteBuilder

Constructors/Destructors

TestSuiteBuilder(TestSuite *suite)
> Constructs a TestSuiteBuilder for a TestSuite.

TestSuiteBuilder(string name)
> Constructs a TestSuiteBuilder and a new TestSuite with the given name.

Public Methods

void addTest(Test *test)
> Adds test to the TestSuite.

void addTestCaller(string methodName, TestMethod testMethod)
> Adds a TestCaller that calls the TestMethod.

void addTestCaller(string methodName, TestMethod testMethod, Fixture *fixture)
> Adds a TestCaller that calls the TestMethod in the context of the Fixture.

template<typename ExceptionType>
> void addTestCallerForException(string methodName, TestMethod testMethod, Fixture *fixture, ExceptionType *dummyPointer)
>> A template function to add a TestCaller that calls the TestMethod in the context of the Fixture. The TestMethod is expected to throw an Exception of type ExceptionType.

string makeTestName(const string &methodName)
>   Returns a test name that incorporates the TestSuite name and methodName.

TestSuite *suite( ) const
>   Returns the TestSuite for this TestSuiteBuilder.

TestSuite *takeSuite( )
>   Takes ownership of the TestSuite from the smart pointer m_suite.

Protected/Private Methods

TestSuite(const TestSuite &other)
>   A copy constructor declared private to prevent its use.

TestSuite& operator=(const TestSuite &other)
>   A copy operator declared private to prevent its use.

Attributes

std::auto_ptr<TestSuite> m_suite
>   A smart pointer to the TestSuite for this TestSuiteBuilder (private).

TestSuiteFactory

Description

The template class TestSuiteFactory (see Figure C-33) implements the TestFactory method makeTest( ) for a TestFixture having a static suite( ) method. TestSuiteFactory is used by the class AutoRegisterSuite.

TestSuiteFactory belongs to the namespace CppUnit. It is declared and implemented in the file *extensions/TestSuiteFactory.h*.

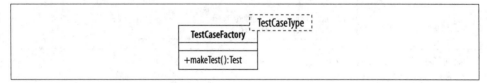

Figure C-33. The template class TestSuiteFactory

Declaration

```
template<typename TestCaseType>
    class TestSuiteFactory : public TestFactory
```

Constructors/Destructors

None.

Public Methods

virtual Test *makeTest( )
>   Calls the method TestCaseType::suite( ) to return a TestSuite.

Protected/Private Methods

None.

Attributes

None.

TextOutputter

Description

The class TextOutputter (see Figure C-34) is a subclass of Outputter. It gets test results from a TestResultCollector and outputs them in text format to an output stream.

TextOutputter belongs to the namespace CppUnit. It is declared in *TextOutputter.h* and implemented in *TextOutputter.cpp*.

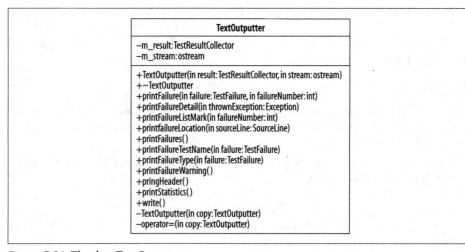

Figure C-34. The class TextOutputter

Declaration

```
class TextOutputter : public Outputter
```

Constructors/Destructors

TextOutputter(TestResultCollector *result, ostream& stream)
    Creates a TextOutputter to get test results from result and output them to stream.
virtual ~TextOutputter()
    A destructor.

Public Methods

```
virtual void printFailure(TestFailure *failure, int failureNumber)
virtual void printFailureDetail(Exception *thrownException)
virtual void printFailureListMark(int failureNumber)
virtual void printFailureLocation(SourceLine sourceLine)
virtual void printFailures()
virtual void printFailureTestName(TestFailure *failure)
virtual void printFailureType(TestFailure *failure)
virtual void printFailureWarning()
virtual void printHeader()
virtual void printStatistics()
```
> Methods that print various portions of the test results to m_stream. Generally, the write() method is called instead of calling these methods directly.

```
void write()
```
> A method called to output results. Calls printHeader() and printFailures().

Protected/Private Methods

```
TextOutputter(const TextOutputter& copy)
```
> A copy constructor, scoped private to prevent its use.

```
void operator=(const TextOutputter& copy)
```
> A copy operator, scoped private to prevent its use.

Attributes

```
TestResultCollector *m_result
```
> The TestResultCollector passed in the constructor. (private)

```
ostream& m_stream
```
> The output stream passed in the constructor. (private)

TextTestProgressListener

Description

The class TextTestProgressListener (see Figure C-35) is a subclass of TestListener. It prints a textual "progress bar" indicating the progress of a series of tests as they are run. A sample of its output is shown here:

```
....F...E...
```

This shows that 10 tests were run, and 1 failure and 1 error occurred.

TextTestProgressListener belongs to the namespace CppUnit. It is declared in *TextTestProgressListener.h* and implemented in *TextTestProgressListener.cpp*.

Declaration

```
class TextTestProgressListener : public TestListener
```

```
                    ┌─────────────────────────────────────────────────────┐
                    │              TextTestProgressListener                │
                    ├─────────────────────────────────────────────────────┤
                    │ +TextTestProgressListener( )                         │
                    │ +~TextTestProgressListener( )                        │
                    │ +addFailure(in failure: TestFailure)                 │
                    │ +done( )                                             │
                    │ +startTest(in test: Test)                            │
                    │ −TextTestProgressListener(in copy: TextTestProgressListener) │
                    │ −operator=(in copy: TextTestProgressListener)        │
                    └─────────────────────────────────────────────────────┘
```

Figure C-35. The class TextTestProgressListener

Constructors/Destructors

TextTestProgressListener( )
> A constructor.

virtual ~TextTestProgressListener( )
> A destructor.

Public Methods

void addFailure(const TestFailure &failure)
> A method that informs TextTestProgressListener of a TestFailure. If the TestFailure is an assertion failure, an F is printed; otherwise, an E is printed.

void done( )
> Prints a carriage return and flushes the output stream to complete the output.

void startTest(Test *test)
> A method that informs TextTestProgressListener that a Test is about to be run. A period (.) is printed to indicate progress.

Protected/Private Methods

TextTestProgressListener(const TextTestProgressListener& copy)
> A copy constructor, scoped private to prevent its use.

void operator=(const TextTestProgressListener& copy)
> A copy operator, scoped private to prevent its use.

Attributes

None.

TextTestResult

Description

This class is deprecated and should not be used. The classes TextTestProgressListener and TextOutputter replace it.

TextTestResult is declared in *TextTestResult.h* and implemented in *TextTestResult.cpp*.

XmlOutputter

Description

The class XmlOutputter (see Figure C-36) is a subclass of Outputter. It gets test results from a TestResultCollector and outputs them in XML format to an output stream. The write( ) method is called to produce the output, rather than calling the other output methods directly.

XmlOutputter defines a nested class named Node representing an XML node.

XmlOutputter belongs to the namespace CppUnit. It is declared in *XmlOutputter.h* and implemented in *XmlOutputter.cpp*.

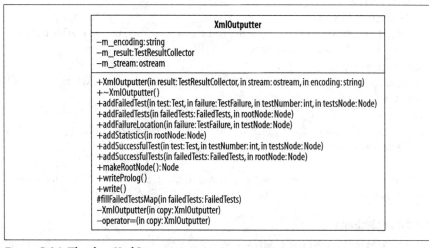

Figure C-36. The class XmlOutputter

Declaration

```
class XmlOutputter : public Outputter
```

Constructors/Destructors

XmlOutputter(TestResultCollector *result, ostream &stream, string encoding = "ISO-8859-1")

>   Constructs an XmlOutputter to get test results from result and output them to stream. The default encoding is ASCII, also known as Latin-1 or ISO 8859-1.

virtual ~XmlOutputter( )

>   A destructor.

Public Methods

virtual void addFailedTest(Test *test, TestFailure *failure, int testNumber, Node *testsNode)

>   Creates an XML node representing the test failure and adds it to testsNode. Also calls addFailureLocation( ) if the test failure has a valid SourceLine.

```
virtual void addFailedTests(FailedTests &failedTests, Node *rootNode)
```
Adds the test failures from failedTests to rootNode using addFailedTest( ).
```
virtual void addFailureLocation(TestFailure *failure, Node *testNode)
```
Creates an XML node representing the test failure location and adds it to testNode.
```
virtual void addStatistics(Node *rootNode)
```
Creates an XML node containing the number of tests, number of failures, and number of errors, and adds it to rootNode.
```
virtual void addSucessfulTest(Test *test, int testNumber, Node *testsNode)
```
Creates an XML node representing a test success and adds it to testsNode.
```
virtual void addSucessfulTests(FailedTests &failedTests, Node *rootNode)
```
Adds the successful tests from the TestResultCollector to rootNode using addSucessfulTest( ).
```
virtual Node *makeRootNode( )
```
Creates a Node and adds the test results to it using addFailedTests( ), addSucessfulTests( ), and addStatistics( ).
```
virtual void writeProlog( )
```
A method that writes the XML prolog (header), which includes the XML version (1.0) and the encoding type.
```
virtual void writeTestsResult( )
```
A method that writes the body of the XML document. Calls makeRootNode( ) and writes the resulting Node to the output stream as a string.
```
void write( )
```
Method called to write the test results to the output stream as an XML document. Calls writeProlog( ) and writeTestsResult( ).

Protected/Private Methods

```
virtual void fillFailedTestsMap(FailedTests &failedTests)
```
A protected method to get the test failures from the TestResultCollector and add them to failedTests.
```
XmlOutputter(const XmlOutputter& copy)
```
A copy constructor, scoped private to prevent its use.
```
void operator=(const XmlOutputter& copy)
```
A copy operator, scoped private to prevent its use.

Attributes

```
typedef map<Test *,TestFailure*> FailedTests
```
Defines the type FailedTests as a map of Test objects to TestFailure objects.
```
string m_encoding
```
The encoding type to be written in the XML prolog (private).
```
TestResultCollector *m_result
```
The TestResultCollector passed in the constructor (private).
```
ostream& m_stream
```
The output stream passed in the constructor (private).

XmlOutputter::Node

Description

The class XmlOutputter::Node (see Figure C-37) is a nested class belonging to XmlOutputter. It represents a node in an XML document.

XmlOutputter::Node is declared in *XmlOutputter.h* and implemented in *XmlOutputter.cpp*.

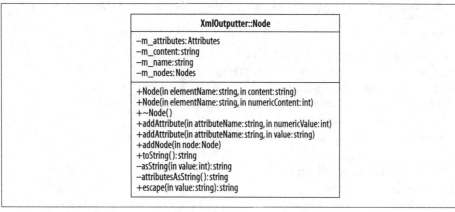

Figure C-37. The nested class XmlOutputter::Node

Declaration

```
class Node
```

Constructors/Destructors

Node(string elementName, string content ="")
  Constructs a Node with the given element name and a string value as content.

Node(string elementName, int numericContent)
  Constructs a Node with the given element name and a numeric value as content.

virtual ~Node( )
  A destructor.

Public Methods

void addAttribute(string attributeName, int numericValue)
  Adds an XML attribute with a numeric value to this Node.

void addAttribute(string attributeName, string value)
  Adds an XML attribute with a string value to this Node.

void addNode(Node *node)
  Adds a child Node to this Node.

string toString( ) const
  Returns the XML-formatted string representation of this Node.

Protected/Private Methods

`static string asString(int value)`
> A Static method that returns a string containing value (private).

`string attributesAsString( ) const`
> Returns this Node's attributes as a string for XML output. (private).

`string escape(string value) const`
> Returns value with certain characters replaced with their XML escaped equivalents. Characters that will be replaced include "<", ">", "&", and quote symbols (private).

Attributes

`typedef std::pair<string,string> Attribute`
> Defines the type Attribute as a pair of strings (private).

`typedef deque<Attribute> Attributes`
> Defines the type Attributes as a deque of Attribute (private).

`typedef deque<Node *> Nodes`
> Defines the type Nodes as a deque of Node (private).

`Attributes m_attributes`
> This Node's attributes (private).

`string m_content`
> The content of this Node (private).

`string m_name`
> The name of this Node (private).

`Nodes m_nodes`
> The child Nodes of this Node (private).

Glossary

abstract

A class is abstract when it cannot be instantiated and so only may be used as a parent class.

Abstract Window Toolkit (AWT)

Java tools for building GUIs.

American Standard Code for Information Interchange (ASCII)

A standard, 8-bit character set containing 127 characters. Also known as Latin-1 and ISO 8859-1.

Application Program Interface (API)

A generic term for a set of software interfaces exposed by a package or standard. For example, DOM is a standard API for accessing document contents.

assert

A method or macro that tests a condition and reports an error if the result is false.

attribute

A variable or constant belonging to a class, representing part of its state. (In .NET, an attribute is metadata containing descriptive declarations and attached to a code element such as a class or method.)

behavior

The results of running code. More formally, how data changes state over time.

black box test

A test that does not have access to the internals of the object being tested. Also known as a "functional test."

coupling

See "test coupling."

Document Object Model (DOM)

A W3C-defined standard interface for document access.

error

In unit testing, an unexpected exception. See "failure."

exception

An error object that is thrown when a software fault occurs.

failure

In unit testing, the result of a test when a test condition does not pass. Failures are expected exceptions. See "error."

fixture

See "test fixture."

functional test

See "black box test."

GNU

GNU's Not Unix, a popular free operating system and associated tools.

green bar

When all unit tests pass.

GUI

Graphical User Interface.

IDE

Integrated Development Environment.

interface

In object-oriented (OO) design, a set of abstract methods that descendant classes will implement (sometimes encapsulated in an abstract class).

isolation

Tests that do not depend on the result of any other test are isolated. See also "test coupling."

iteration

A software development cycle. Iterations start with a set of stories and finish with working software that implements those stories.

Java API for XML Processing (JAXP)

Java's generic interface for parsing and transforming XML documents. It is implemented by numerous different XML tools, including Crimson, Xerces, and Xalan. It incorporates other industry standard APIs such as DOM and SAX.

macro

A command embedded in code that is executed by the compiler prior to compiling the code.

member

A method or attribute belonging to a class.

method

A function belonging to a class.

Microsoft Foundation Classes (MFC)

A set of standard C++ classes for building Microsoft Windows applications.

mock object

A simulation of a real object that implements its interface and validates its interaction with other objects.

MUTual EXclusion object (mutex)

A mechanism that may be locked and unlocked to protect a synchronized object.

nested class

A class defined within another class.

object

An element of code structured as a class.

Object Oriented (OO)

Code structured with classes.

pair programing

Developers writing code in teams of two, a common XP practice.

private

A class member that is only accessible by the owning class.

production class

An object that will be included in the delivered software product. See "test class."

protected

A class member with access limited to the owning class, child classes, and friend classes.

public

A class member that any other class can access.

pure virtual

A method with no implementation that must be overridden in a subclass.

Quality assurance (QA)

Formal verification of software by both automated and manual testing.

Qt

A cross-platform C++ GUI development framework.

red bar

When one or more unit tests fail.

refactoring

The process of transforming code to improve its internal design without changing its external functionality. More succinctly, a behavior-preserving transformation.

reflection

Reading the structure of a class at runtime.

Simple API for XML (SAX)

An older standard interface for XML handling.

singleton

An object that has one, and only one, global instance.

structural test

See "white box test."

success

In unit testing, the result of a test when all test conditions pass.

Swing

Java tools for GUI building, a later extension of AWT.

TDD

Test Driven Development.

template

In C++, a parameterized class. Must be specialized for a particular data type to be instantiated.

test class

Object implementing unit test(s). Generally not included in the software product. See "production class."

test coupling

Tests that depend on the results of another test are coupled. See "isolation."

test fixture

A unit test containing objects that are shared by two or more test methods.

test method

A test function within a test class that produces a result of either success or failure.

Transformation API for XML (TrAX)

The API for XML document transformation included within JAXP.

UI

User interface.

Unified Modeling Language (UML)

A standard language for documenting and modeling software architecture.

Uniform Resource Locator (URL)

A string describing the location and access method of a network resource—for example, *http://www.oreilly.com*.

unit test

A test of a software component or behavior.

unit test framework

A software tool that supports writing and running unit tests.

virtual

A method that is meant to be overridden. See also "pure virtual."

World Wide Web Consortium (W3C)

An organization that defines web-related specifications, guidelines, software, and tools such as XML and HTML.

white box test

A test that has access to the internals of the object being tested. Also known as a "structural test."

Extensible Markup Language (XML)

A metalanguage for defining customized markup formats for documents.

XP

Extreme Programming.

XPath

A W3C Recommendation specifying a standard path language for querying and manipulating XML documents.

XSL

A set of recommendations for defining XML document transformation and presentation.

Index

We'd like to hear your suggestions for improving our indexes. Send email to *index@oreilly.com.*

About the Author

Paul Hamill first programmed on a PDP-11 in the early 1980s and has been writing code ever since, working on many software projects large and small, for customers ranging from Fortune 500 corporations to startups. Paul's technical interests include Agile Development and advanced GUIs and graphics. He holds a BS in mechanical engineering from Cornell University and an MS in electrical engineering from the University of Colorado at Boulder. Along with his wonderful wife, Anya, amazing son, Pavel, and brave dog, Sputnik, he makes his home in Boulder, Colorado.

Colophon

Our look is the result of reader comments, our own experimentation, and feedback from distribution channels. Distinctive covers complement our distinctive approach to technical topics, breathing personality and life into potentially dry subjects.

The animal on the cover of *Unit Test Frameworks* is a Norway rat. Contrary to its name, the Norway rat's origins are in Asia; over the centuries, it has spread throughout the world. It is often blamed for transmitting the Black Plague through Europe, but another species, the black rat, is actually responsible for this. The Norway rat's appearance includes a brown or dark gray coat with a white or grayish underside, pointed ears, a long snout, and a scaly tail. It averages about 9 to 10 inches in length. It builds its own nest of twigs and leaves and is mostly nocturnal. It makes its habitat where food is most accessible and is typically found in cities, where it can root through garbage; near farms where it can forage through the harvest; and near the ocean, where it can eat fish, seaweed, and the like. It lives among large groups of other rats, usually with one male designated as the leader.

Along with the common house mouse, the Norway rat is the most popular animal model for scientific lab testing. (The lab rats are usually albino, however.) It is useful because its metabolism is very much like a human's and the rats often are affected by the same diseases and sicknesses as humans.

Mary Brady was the production editor and the copyeditor for *Unit Test Frameworks*. Colleen Gorman proofread the book. Matt Hutchinson and Claire Cloutier provided quality control. Ellen Troutman-Zaig wrote the index.

Ellie Volckhausen designed the cover of this book, based on a series design by Edie Freedman. The cover image is a 19th-century engraving from the Dover Pictorial Archive. Clay Fernald produced the cover layout with QuarkXPress 4.1 using Adobe's ITC Garamond font. David Futato designed and produced the CD label using Adobe InDesign CS.

Melanie Wang designed the interior layout, based on a series design by David Futato. This book was converted by Julie Hawks to FrameMaker 5.5.6 with a format conversion tool created by Erik Ray, Jason McIntosh, Neil Walls, and Mike Sierra that uses Perl and XML technologies. The text font is Linotype Birka; the heading font is Adobe Myriad Condensed; and the code font is LucasFont's TheSans Mono Condensed. The illustrations that appear in the book were produced by Robert Romano and Jessamyn Read using Macromedia FreeHand MX and Adobe Photoshop CS. This colophon was written by Mary Brady.

Better than e-books

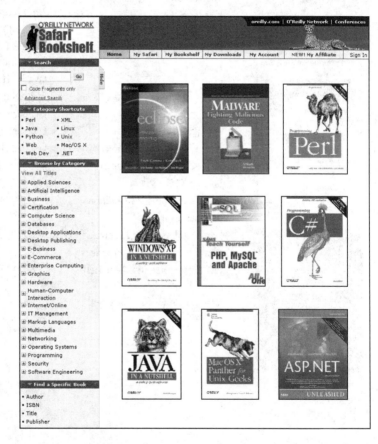

Search
inside electronic versions of thousands of books

Browse
books by category. With Safari researching any topic is a snap

Find
answers in an instant

Read books from cover to cover. Or, simply click to the page you need.

Search Safari! The premier electronic reference library for programmers and IT professionals

Related Titles Available from O'Reilly

Java

Ant: The Definitive Guide

Better, Faster, Lighter Java

Eclipse

Eclipse Cookbook

Enterprise JavaBeans,
4th Edition

Hardcore Java

Head First Java

Head First Servlets & JSP

Head First EJB

Hibernate:
A Developer's Notebook

J2EE Design Patterns

Java 1.5 Tiger:
A Developer's Notebook

Java & XML Data Binding

Java & XML

Java Cookbook, *2nd Edition*

Java Data Objects

Java Database Best Practices

Java Enterprise Best Practices

Java Enterprise in a Nutshell,
2nd Edition

Java Examples in a Nutshell,
3rd Edition

Java Extreme Programming
Cookbook

Java in a Nutshell, *4th Edition*

Java Management Extensions

Java Message Service

Java Network Programming,
2nd Edition

Java NIO

Java Performance Tuning,
2nd Edition

Java RMI

Java Security, *2nd Edition*

JavaServer Faces

Java ServerPages, *2nd Edition*

Java Servlet & JSP Cookbook

Java Servlet Programming,
2nd Edition

Java Swing, *2nd Edition*

Java Web Services in a Nutshell

Learning Java, *2nd Edition*

Mac OS X for Java Geeks

Programming Jakarta Struts
2nd Edition

Tomcat: The Definitive Guide

WebLogic:
The Definitive Guide

O'REILLY®

Our books are available at most retail and online bookstores.
To order direct: 1-800-998-9938 • *order@oreilly.com* • *www.oreilly.com*
Online editions of most O'Reilly titles are available by subscription at *safari.oreilly.com*

Keep in touch with O'Reilly

1. Download examples from our books

To find example files for a book, go to:

www.oreilly.com/catalog

select the book, and follow the "Examples" link.

2. Register your O'Reilly books

Register your book at *register.oreilly.com*

Why register your books?
Once you've registered your O'Reilly books you can:

- Win O'Reilly books, T-shirts or discount coupons in our monthly drawing.
- Get special offers available only to registered O'Reilly customers.
- Get catalogs announcing new books (US and UK only).
- Get email notification of new editions of the O'Reilly books you own.

3. Join our email lists

Sign up to get topic-specific email announcements of new books and conferences, special offers, and O'Reilly Network technology newsletters at:

elists.oreilly.com

It's easy to customize your free elists subscription so you'll get exactly the O'Reilly news you want.

4. Get the latest news, tips, and tools

www.oreilly.com

- "Top 100 Sites on the Web"—PC Magazine
- CIO Magazine's Web Business 50 Awards

Our web site contains a library of comprehensive product information (including book excerpts and tables of contents), downloadable software, background articles, interviews with technology leaders, links to relevant sites, book cover art, and more.

5. Work for O'Reilly

Check out our web site for current employment opportunities:

jobs.oreilly.com

6. Contact us

O'Reilly & Associates
1005 Gravenstein Hwy North
Sebastopol, CA 95472 USA

TEL: 707-827-7000 or 800-998-9938
(6am to 5pm PST)

FAX: 707-829-0104

order@oreilly.com
For answers to problems regarding your order or our products. To place a book order online, visit:

www.oreilly.com/order_new

catalog@oreilly.com
To request a copy of our latest catalog.

booktech@oreilly.com
For book content technical questions or corrections.

corporate@oreilly.com
For educational, library, government, and corporate sales.

proposals@oreilly.com
To submit new book proposals to our editors and product managers.

international@oreilly.com
For information about our international distributors or translation queries. For a list of our distributors outside of North America check out:

international.oreilly.com/distributors.html

adoption@oreilly.com
For information about academic use of O'Reilly books, visit:

academic.oreilly.com

O'REILLY®

Our books are available at most retail and online bookstores.
To order direct: 1-800-998-9938 • *order@oreilly.com* • *www.oreilly.com*
Online editions of most O'Reilly titles are available by subscription at *safari.oreilly.com*